P9-DBQ-124

Grand Diplôme Cooking Course

Volume 5

Grand Diplôme Cooking Course

A Danbury Press Book

The Danbury Press

a division of Grolier Enterprises, Inc.

Robert B. Clarke Publisher

This book has been adapted from the Grand Diplôme Cooking Course, originally published by Purnell Cookery, U.S.A.

Library of Congress Catalog Card Number: 72-13896

Filmsetting by Petty and Sons Ltd., Leeds, England.
Printed in the United States of America

345678998

All recipes have been tested either at the Cordon Bleu Cookery School in London or in our U.S. test kitchens.

Note: all recipe quantities in this book serve 4 people unless otherwise stated.

Contents

From the Editor

Full-bodied fragrant sauerbraten or regal salmon stuffed with truffles – the techniques of **Braising** and **Marinating** are an open book in this Volume of your Grand Diplôme Cooking Course, created by the London Cordon Bleu Cookery School. Take a Dutch oven, a skillet and a sharp knife and you're all set for a **Cook's Vacation** of easy, one-dish entrées and desserts. Or stay at home and let your palate take a vacation – transport your taste buds to Turkey, your palate to Paris, your imagination to the Mediterranean with some **Around the World Dishes** off the culinary track. Pause in Italy and sample its slender spaghetti or lengthy linguine – you'll find **Cooking with Pasta** offers innumerable opportunities to display your Grand Diplôme skills.

Gather home for the harvest of **Apples and Pears** – these everyday fruits are given a distinctive touch in desserts like Eve's pudding and pears poached in red wine. Reminisce with an old friend, the worthy **Waffle**, as it takes a foreign flair in Belgian gaufrettes, Norwegian goro and Swedish sockerstruvor rosettes. Spend a delectable sojourn discovering the versatility of **Eggs**, as they blossom at brunch in béchamel sauce, hide behind a mask of spinach soufflé at dinner or star at the supper table baked with sausage, peas and peppers in flamboyant Flamenco style.

The teenagers will take to the kitchen themselves with a series of simple **Menus** based on fondue bourguignonne or the ever-popular hamburger. And then for more elegant entertaining, try a dinner featuring duck in a rich wine sauce, with succulent oranges en surprise, filled with fruit salad and ice cream and topped with melting meringue.

Exotic though they may be, you'll find all of these exciting dishes are at home in your kitchen so, Bon Appétit!

Anne Willan

Start your menu

Fillets of sole mornay are lightly browned, then garnished with cucumber bâtons (recipe is on page 10)

with sole or soup

Serve a simple menu of tomato soup refreshed with orange, followed by leg of lamb with a touch of spice, and an apricot gelatin dessert. Or, if you're feeling more festive, start the meal with sole mornay – fresh fillets of sole in a delicious cheese-flavored sauce.

The ideal wine partner for lamb is a classic, dry red from Bordeaux. By general agreement, the best of these wines hail from the Médoc district: St. Julien is suggested because its full, rich aroma and flavor is well suited to this piquant lamb dish. The Cabernet Sauvignon, made chiefly from the same grape used in St. Julien, is unquestionably America's top red wine when raised in the better California vineyards.

Fillets of Sole Mornay
or
Tomato & Orange Soup

Spiced Leg of Lamb
Potato & Mushroom Casserole
or
Boiled New Potatoes
Orange, Lettuce & Onion Salad

Apricot Suédoise with Meringues

Red wine – St. Julien (Bordeaux)
or Cabernet Sauvignon (California)

TIMETABLE

Day before
Make meringues for suédoise and store in an airtight container.
Rub dry seasonings into leg of lamb and refrigerate. Make stock for gravy *and soup*, cover and chill. Make spiced sauce mixture and keep covered.
Make soup and keep in refrigerator.

Morning
Make suédoise, cover tightly and chill.
Prepare orange rind for soup and keep covered.
Make potato and mushroom casserole and leave in pot ready for reheating.
Peel or scrub new potatoes and keep in cold water.
Make mornay sauce for fish, cover tightly and refrigerate. Make cucumber bâtons and keep covered.
Chop parsley for garnish.
Section oranges and keep covered; make salad dressing, leaving out mint.

Assemble equipment for final cooking from 6:00 for dinner around 8 p.m.

Order of Work

6:00
Set oven at hot (400°F).
Insert garlic slivers in the leg of lamb.
Wash fillets of sole, dry and arrange in baking dish; cover with buttered foil.

6:15
Put lamb in oven and baste well.
Whip cream for suédoise; unmold dessert, decorate and chill.

6:45
Baste the lamb.

7:15
Turn down oven to moderately hot (375°F). Pour fat from roasting pan, turn lamb, add half the spiced sauce and continue cooking.

7:30
Baste lamb with the remaining spiced sauce.
Put sole in oven; gently reheat mornay sauce. Cook cucumber bâtons and keep warm.
Boil new potatoes; slice onions for the salad.

7:45
Take lamb from oven, transfer to a platter and keep warm. Make gravy, strain and keep hot. Put potato and mushroom casserole in a water bath to reheat *or drain new potatoes, and complete orange and onion salad.*
Transfer sole to a platter, finish mornay sauce, coat fish and broil until browned; add cucumber garnish. *Or reheat soup and add cream and orange strips.*

8:00
Serve sole mornay *or soup. Toss new potatoes in butter and parsley just before serving.*

Appetizer

Fillets of Sole Mornay

1–1½ lb fillets of sole
salt
1 small onion, sliced
6 peppercorns
½ bay leaf
6 tablespoons water

For mornay sauce
2 tablespoons butter
2 tablespoons flour
1¼ cups milk
salt and pepper
3 tablespoons grated Swiss or Parmesan cheese

On the East Coast you can find true Channel or Dover sole, imported from England, Belgium, the Netherlands and Denmark. It generally comes frozen and is expensive.

The nearest equivalent fish found in American waters is gray or lemon sole, but it doesn't compare in texture or flavor with European sole. In any of our recipes for sole, like this one, you can use flounder fillets.

Method
Wash fillets and dry with paper towels. Fold the ends of each fillet under so they all appear to be the same size and put them in a shallow baking dish. Sprinkle with a little salt and add onion slices, peppercorns, bay leaf and the water. Cover with buttered paper and bake 10–12 minutes in a moderate oven (350°F) or until the fish flakes easily.

To prepare mornay sauce: melt 2 tablespoons butter in a saucepan, remove from heat, blend in flour and pour on the milk. Season lightly with salt and pepper, return sauce to the heat and bring slowly to a boil, stirring constantly. Strain all liquid from the fish, add it to the sauce and cook 2–3 minutes longer. Remove sauce from the heat and stir in the cheese, a little at a time, reserving 1 tablespoon. Arrange fish in a gratin or flameproof serving dish, cover with sauce and sprinkle with the reserved cheese. Brown the dish lightly under the broiler. Garnish with cucumber bâtons.

Cucumber Bâtons
Trim the ends from 2 cucumbers, peel them thinly, and cut in half lengthwise; scrape out the seeds with the tip of a teaspoon and discard. Cut the halves into small sticks about 2 inches long, shaping the sticks to a point at each end. Cook in boiling salted water for 3–5 minutes or until almost tender. Drain the sticks (bâtons) thoroughly, toss in 3 tablespoons melted butter and 1 tablespoon chopped parsley, with salt and pepper to taste.

You will find that **cooking times** given in the individual recipes for these dishes have sometimes been adapted in the timetable to help you when cooking and serving them as a party meal.

Alternative appetizer

Tomato and Orange Soup

6 tomatoes
rind and juice of $\frac{1}{2}$ orange
1 onion, sliced
1 carrot, sliced
strip of lemon rind
1 bay leaf
6 peppercorns
salt and pepper
4 cups chicken stock
3 tablespoons butter
3–4 tablespoons flour
sugar (to taste)
$\frac{1}{2}$ cup light cream

Method
Wash tomatoes, remove the cores and cut in half. Squeeze them gently to remove the seeds. Put tomatoes, onion and carrot in a saucepan with lemon rind, bay leaf, peppercorns and a good pinch of salt. Add stock to tomato mixture, cover and simmer about 30 minutes, or until the tomatoes are pulpy. Work the mixture through a sieve or food mill and set it aside.

Wipe out the pan, melt butter in it and stir in the flour. Pour in tomato mixture, stir well and bring to a boil. Cut orange rind into fine strips, blanch it by cooking in boiling water for 5 minutes, drain and rinse well with cold water. Set aside. Add orange juice to the soup, with seasoning and sugar to taste. Just before serving stir in cream and orange rind. Serve at once.

Use fresh tomatoes, onion, carrot and lemon rind, together with herbs and other seasonings for making tomato and orange soup

The completed dinner includes orange and tomato soup, spiced leg of lamb and apricot suédoise

Entrée

Spiced Leg of Lamb

$3\frac{1}{2}$–4 lb leg of lamb
$2\frac{1}{2}$ cups water (for stock)
1 small onion, quartered (for stock)
1 teaspoon salt
1 teaspoon dry mustard
1 teaspoon sugar
1 teaspoon freshly ground black pepper
1 teaspoon ground ginger
2 tablespoons oil
1 large clove of garlic
1 tablespoon flour
2 teaspoons arrowroot mixed to a paste with 2 tablespoons stock

For spiced sauce
2 tablespoons ketchup
2 tablespoons Worcestershire sauce
2 tablespoons currant, or plum, jam or jelly
2–3 tablespoons melted butter
1 teaspoon sugar
dash of red wine vinegar
dash of Tabasco

This dish must be started the day before serving to give the dry seasonings time to flavor the meat.

Method
To make the stock: cut off the shank end of leg (the butcher usually saws through the bone), put it into a pan with water and onion, and simmer 45 minutes. Strain and reserve this stock for gravy.

Mix the dry seasonings together, rub the mixture all over the leg of lamb, cover and leave overnight in the refrigerator.

Heat the oil in a roasting pan, peel and split the garlic clove in 4–5 pieces and stick these into the lean meat of the leg, near the bone. Sprinkle the lamb with flour, put it in the hot roasting pan and brush the surface with hot oil. Roast 1 hour in a hot oven (400°F), basting and turning the meat from time to time.

To make the spiced sauce: mix together ketchup, Worcestershire sauce, and jam or jelly. Stir the mixture into the melted butter with sugar, vinegar and Tabasco.

Remove the lamb from the oven and discard the fat from the pan. Pour half the spiced sauce over the meat. Reduce the oven heat to moderately hot (375°F) and continue roasting for 15 minutes. Baste the meat with remaining sauce. If the roasting pan is dry, add 2–3 tablespoons of the prepared stock to keep the meat moist. Continue roasting 15–20 minutes longer. Transfer lamb to a warm platter and keep warm.

To make the gravy: pour the prepared stock into the roasting pan and boil it well until reduced to about $1\frac{1}{2}$ cups. Thicken by whisking in the arrowroot paste and bringing it to a boil; taste for seasoning, strain and serve in a gravy boat.

As an accompaniment to this dish make potato and mushroom casserole, or serve boiled new potatoes, and a salad of orange, lettuce and onion.

Accompaniment to entrée

Potato and Mushroom Casserole

$1\frac{1}{2}$ lb new potatoes
2 cups ($\frac{1}{2}$ lb) mushrooms
2 tablespoons butter
2 tablespoons flour
$2\frac{1}{2}$ cups milk
salt and pepper
1–2 tablespoons heavy cream
pinch of nutmeg

This dish is best made with small new potatoes, but regular potatoes can be substituted.

Method
Peel potatoes and, if large, cut each one in quarters, trimming the cut edges with a potato peeler. Cook the potatoes in boiling, salted water for 10–15 minutes (depending on their age) until almost tender. Drain, let stand over a gentle heat to dry; cover and set aside.

Wipe the mushrooms with a damp cloth and trim each stem level with the base of the cap.

Watchpoint: be careful not to pull out the whole stems or the mushrooms will shrink and lose their form during cooking. The little piece of remaining stem keeps the mushroom in shape.

Melt the butter, add mushrooms, and toss over a high heat until soft. Stir in the flour, remove from heat, add milk and seasonings, then cook, stirring constantly, until mixture boils. Add potatoes, cover, and simmer 10 minutes. Shortly before serving stir in the cream and a pinch of nutmeg.

Alternative accompaniment

Orange, Lettuce and Onion Salad

6 navel oranges
1 head Boston or 2 heads Bibb lettuce
1 red onion, very thinly sliced

For dressing
6 tablespoons oil
2 tablespoons lime juice
1 tablespoon chopped mint
salt and pepper

If you choose sole mornay as the appetizer for this menu to avoid serving two white sauces, substitute orange, lettuce and onion salad and boiled new potatoes for potato and mushroom casserole.

Method
Wash the lettuce and dry thoroughly. Peel the oranges, removing all the skin, and section them.

To make the dressing, beat all the ingredients together with a whisk until slightly thickened.

On four individual salad plates arrange lettuce leaves with the orange sections and onion slices overlapping on top. Spoon over the dressing just before serving.

Apricot Suédoise with Meringues

$\frac{1}{2}$ lb (1$\frac{1}{2}$ cups) dried apricots (soaked, if necessary)
strip of lemon rind
2$\frac{1}{4}$ cups water
$\frac{1}{2}$ cup sugar
2 envelopes gelatin
$\frac{1}{2}$ cup heavy cream, whipped until it holds a soft shape
$\frac{1}{2}$ teaspoon vanilla

For meringues
2 egg whites
$\frac{1}{2}$ cup sugar

6 inch soufflé dish, or deep cake pan (1$\frac{1}{2}$ quart capacity); pastry bag and $\frac{1}{4}$ inch plain tube (optional)

Method

Soak apricots if necessary according to package directions, then cook them with lemon rind in 2 cups water until very soft. Work apricots and their liquid through a sieve, or remove the lemon rind and purée them in a blender. Add enough water to make 4 cups of the mixture. Return it to the pan with the sugar and simmer 5 minutes. In a small pan sprinkle gelatin over remaining $\frac{1}{4}$ cup water and leave 5 minutes or until spongy. Stir it into the hot apricot purée and cool, continuing to stir occasionally. Pour into the soufflé dish or cake pan; chill for several hours until firmly set.

To prepare the meringues: beat the egg whites until they hold a stiff peak. Beat in 1 heaping tablespoon of the sugar and continue beating for about 1 minute or until the mixture is very glossy. Fold in the remaining sugar with a metal spoon.

Spoon little mounds of the meringue onto a baking sheet covered with silicone paper, making them the size of a half dollar. Alternatively, pipe the meringue into little mounds, using a pastry bag fitted with a plain tube.

Bake meringues in a low oven (250°F) for about 45 minutes, or until they are dry and crisp. Just before serving, turn the apricot mold onto a platter. Flavor the lightly-whipped cream with vanilla and spread over the mold. Then attach meringues to the entire surface.

Suédoise usually means a sweet fruit purée set with gelatin and then molded. It is served with cream or custard.

Pipe the meringues onto a lined baking sheet using a pastry bag fitted with a $\frac{1}{4}$ inch plain tube

Apricot suédoise, a fruit purée gelatin, is spread with whipped cream and decorated with meringues

Leftover Meringues

If you like to make double quantity of meringues, they keep well in an airtight tin for 4–6 weeks.

Large or small meringues can be sandwiched with Chantilly cream (see page 107) to serve alone or with a fruit sauce. Large meringues can also be sandwiched with ice cream and served with hot chocolate sauce (see Volume 1).

For a special occasion, spread a layer of softened strawberry or chocolate ice cream in a springform pan and cover with crushed meringues. Chill until firm and add a layer of softened vanilla ice cream and another layer of meringue. Chill until firm and fill the mold with another layer of strawberry or chocolate ice cream and chill again. The cake can be stored in the freezer for up to 2 months. Just before serving, unmold it onto a platter, stick tiny meringues around the edge (as for apricot suédoise) and serve with chilled Melba sauce (for strawberry cake – see Volume 3) or hot chocolate sauce (for chocolate cake).

COOKING WITH EGGS

Eggs are perhaps the most valuable of all basic cooking ingredients. High in protein, they can provide a quick nutritious meal and there are many more ways to cook them than just boiling, frying or scrambling. Eat eggs when they are as fresh as possible. You can easily recognize a freshly laid egg (up to one week old): when it is broken, the white will cling to the yolk. To test for freshness without first breaking the egg: shake it – fresh ones should feel heavy and well filled. Egg shells are porous and a certain amount of liquid evaporates every day, resulting in a lighter egg.

Eggs are sold in many sizes and an egg called for in a recipe is assumed to be the 2 oz size classed as 'large'. Proportions of a recipe can be greatly altered by using larger or smaller eggs so it is important to use the right size, particularly when baking.

Eggs are delicate and they cook at a lower temperature than most other foods. High heat will make them rubbery – 'boiled' eggs should really be simmered as boiling toughens the whites. They also cook quickly and 20 seconds can make the difference between an egg that is perfectly cooked and one that is overdone.

BASIC METHODS

Boiled Eggs
(Oeufs à la Coque)

'She can't even boil an egg' is not as absurd as it sounds because there is quite an art to cooking an egg. Many things can go wrong: the white may be too soft, the yolk too set or, worst of all, the shell may crack in the water so that some white escapes.

Points to remember

1 Use an enamel or nonstick pan as the eggs will darken an aluminum one. If you do use an aluminum pan, add a little vinegar to the water to help prevent staining. Vinegar will also help prevent the white from leaking if the eggs crack.
2 Never take the eggs straight from the refrigerator but let them stand at room temperature before putting them into boiling salted water.
3 The shells must be perfectly clean. If not, wipe them with a damp cloth.
4 Simmer the eggs gently but steadily for $3\frac{1}{2}$–4 minutes for a lightly cooked egg; simmer 4–$4\frac{1}{2}$ minutes for one that is firmly set (difference in timing largely depends on the freshness of the egg). Count the time from when the water reboils after the eggs are put into the pan.
5 Alternatively, the eggs may be cooked slowly to make the whites more digestible: put them in a pan of cold water, bring slowly to a boil and simmer them gently for 30 seconds and they will be lightly cooked.

Coddled Eggs

Put eggs in a pan of boiling water, cover them, take from heat and leave 5 minutes. Eggs cooked in this way have a soft, creamy white.

If you have no timer, lift eggs from the water and count to 8. If the shell dries, the egg is coddled; if not, replace in pan and cook 30 seconds longer.

Soft-cooked Eggs
(Oeufs Mollets)

Many hot and cold dishes can be made from eggs simmered until the white is firm enough to peel off the shell although the yolk remains soft. This method is slightly different from cooking 4-minute boiled eggs.

Points to remember

1 Put the eggs into a pan of boiling water and simmer them gently, allowing 5 minutes from the time the water comes back to a boil. A small egg will take less. time to cook than a large one.
2 Take eggs out as soon as they are cooked and put into cold water for 7–8 minutes. Peel and use the eggs cold or reheat by putting them, unpeeled, into fairly hot (not boiling) water for 5 minutes. Then peel and use at once.
3 These eggs must be peeled carefully. First, crack the shells all over with the back of a spoon – this softens the shell and makes it easier to remove without breaking the egg – cold running water helps to loosen the shell. Once cracked, peel a band across the middle; the shell at each end pulls off easily.

Hard-cooked or Hard-boiled Eggs
(Oeufs Durs)

Put the eggs in boiling water and simmer 10–12 minutes but no longer. Overcooking produces a black line around the yolks and toughens the whites. Plunge the eggs at once into cold water – this helps prevent overcooking and the black line, and makes them easier to peel (although some eggs are hard to peel under any treatment because of the diet of the hens). Peel them as for soft-cooked eggs.

To stuff hard-cooked eggs

Cut them lengthwise after peeling and scoop out the yolks with the handle of a teaspoon. Put the whites at once into a bowl of cold water to keep them tender and white.

When needed, carefully lift out the whites and lay them, cut side down, on a cloth or paper towel to drain. If serving cold stuffed eggs, arrange the halved whites in place on the platter before filling with the prepared mixture; stick them to the dish with a little of the yolk filling.

An alternative way of arranging the halved whites is to fill them and put them together to reshape the egg. Garnish and serve in same way as halved eggs.

If coating eggs with a sauce, dry them well on a cloth or paper towel so sauce will adhere. Sauce, particularly mayonnaise, should be of a good coating consistency. If finished eggs are to be coated with sauce and browned in the oven or under the broiler, the filling should be of a softer consistency.

Scrambled or Buttered Eggs
(Oeufs Brouillés)

Scrambled eggs may be set or runny, according to your taste, but they should always be soft, creamy and melting in texture. This depends on the amount of butter added and how slowly they are cooked. Do not add too much milk or cream as this can make eggs curdled and watery.

Beat 6 eggs with a fork to mix them well, then beat in $\frac{1}{4}$ cup light cream, or half and half, with salt and pepper to taste and 2 tablespoons butter in small pieces.

Melt another tablespoon butter in a heavy-based or nonstick pan, add the egg mixture and cook over very gentle heat, stirring continuously and scraping the mixture from the bottom with a spoon as it becomes thick and creamy. Take the pan from the heat just before the eggs are done to your taste, as they will continue cooking a few moments in the hot pan. Spoon them onto buttered toast and serve at once.

An alternative method gives a mixture which is not so rich: in the saucepan combine 4–5 tablespoons light cream, or half and half, with 3 tablespoons butter. When hot, break in 6 eggs and allow the whites to set lightly before stirring. Then season and stir the mixture to break up eggs, and continue cooking until the eggs are thickened to your taste.

Note: some cooks like to make scrambled eggs in a double boiler, but this is not necessary if the heat is kept as low as possible.

Poached Eggs
(Oeufs Pochés)

Unless poached eggs are cooked carefully, the white has a tendency to detach itself from the yolk in untidy strings. If possible, use freshly laid eggs so that the white and yolk cling together well. Egg poachers are available but the eggs sometimes stick unless the poachers are well buttered beforehand, so it is best to use one of the following two methods.

1 Fill a shallow saucepan or deep skillet two-thirds full with boiling water, adding about 1 tablespoon vinegar (to help coagulate the white quickly around the yolk) to each quart of water. Do not add salt as this tends to toughen the egg whites.

Bring the water to a rolling boil and break an egg into a briskly bubbling patch – the bubbles will spin the egg so the white sets around the yolk. Repeat with up to 4 more eggs, then turn down the heat at once and simmer the eggs very gently for 3–4 minutes until the whites are firm and the yolks still soft. Lift out the eggs with a slotted spoon and drain thoroughly.

2 With the following method the eggs are well shaped, plump and round, but it takes longer than the previous method as only 1 egg can cook at a time.

Fill a deep saucepan two-thirds full with water and vinegar (1 tablespoon to each quart of water), and bring to a boil. Turn down the heat and, when the water is gently simmering, stir so it forms a whirlpool in the center. Drop an egg into the whirlpool and the action of the water will bring the white up, over and around the yolk. Simmer gently for $3\frac{1}{2}$–$4\frac{1}{2}$ minutes and lift out.

Poached eggs, like soft-cooked (mollet) eggs, can be kept several hours in a bowl of cold water before use. To reheat the eggs, lift them into a bowl of fairly hot (not boiling) water and leave 4–5 minutes. Take them out, trim them and drain well on paper towels.

For cold poached eggs, simply take them out of cold water, trim and dry them. The whites must be really firm and the yolks should just give under gentle pressure.

For hot poached eggs to be served under a sauce the eggs should be slightly softer, especially when they are to be browned in the oven or under the broiler. Be sure the eggs are dry before coating or the sauce will slide off.

Fried Eggs
(Oeufs Frits)

Eggs can be fried in shallow or deep fat.

For shallow fat frying: in a skillet or frying pan heat one-quarter to three-eighths inch layer of fat (preferably butter or bacon fat). Do not let it become too hot or it will toughen the egg whites. Break the eggs, one at a time, into a cup and gently slide them into the pan. Cook over moderate heat, basting with the fat, until both the white and yolk are set.

For deep fat frying: half fill a small deep pan with fat, put in a fat thermometer and heat to 400°F (if using oil, heat only to 360°F–375°F). Break the eggs, one by one, into a cup and gently tip them into the hot fat; cook 2–3 minutes until golden brown. Lift out the eggs with a slotted spoon and drain them thoroughly on paper towels. For best results, do not fry more than two at a time.

Baked or Shirred Eggs
(Oeufs en Cocotte or Oeufs Sur-le-plat)

These delicious and simple eggs may be cooked and served in individual heatproof buttered ramekins, cocottes, custard cups or in shallow baking dishes.

For simple baked eggs: butter the dishes, sprinkle with salt and pepper and break in the eggs. Spoon over a little melted butter and cream and bake in a moderately hot oven (375°F) for 6–8 minutes or until the whites are set and the yolks are still soft.

For a more substantial dish – and an excellent way of using up leftovers – break eggs onto a layer of savory mixture spread in the baking dish.

If the eggs are cooked in shallow flamepoof dishes, cooking may be started over direct heat. When the white begins to set, finish baking in the oven for 4–5 minutes.

Watchpoint: do not overcook as baked eggs continue cooking after the dish has been taken from the oven.

HOT EGG DISHES

The following recipes serve 4 people as a light entrée.

Eggs Beurre Noir

(poached eggs)

8 eggs
8 slices of bread, fried in 4–6 tablespoons oil and butter, mixed (for croûtes), or 8 slices of buttered toast
6 tablespoons butter
2 tablespoons chopped parsley
1 tablespoon chopped gherkin pickles
1 tablespoon capers
salt and pepper
3 tablespoons wine vinegar

The tart but buttery sauce in this recipe makes an excellent contrast to the poached eggs.

Method

Poach the eggs, drain well, and place each one on a croûte or slice of buttered toast. Arrange on a hot platter.

Heat the 6 tablespoons butter in a skillet and cook slowly to a deep nut-brown. At once add the parsley, gherkin pickles, capers, and salt and pepper to taste and pour over the eggs. Add the vinegar to the pan, boil to reduce by half and sprinkle it over the eggs.

Serve with boiled potatoes and green salad.

Push out onion rings to make garnish for eggs soubise

Eggs Soubise

(poached eggs)

8 eggs
2 large Bermuda onions
little egg white
$\frac{1}{4}$ cup seasoned flour (made with $\frac{1}{4}$ teaspoon salt and pinch of pepper)
deep fat (for frying)

For soubise sauce
2 cups chopped onions
5 tablespoons butter
3 tablespoons flour
3 cups milk
salt and pepper

This is one of the best hot egg dishes. The creamy sauce provides a pleasant contrast to the crisp brown onion rings.

Method

To make the soubise sauce: blanch the chopped onions in boiling water for 1 minute, drain well and cook over low heat in 2 tablespoons of the butter until soft but not brown. Work through a sieve or purée in a blender.

Melt the remaining butter in a pan, stir in flour off the heat and pour on the milk. Bring to a boil, stirring, and add onion purée. Simmer 4–5 minutes or until creamy, add salt and pepper to taste and keep warm.

Slice the other onions and push out into rings. Slightly beat the egg white, and toss onion rings in it to coat them. Toss well in seasoned flour and fry the rings in hot deep fat (375°F on a fat thermometer) until crisp and lightly golden. Drain well on paper towels and keep hot.

Poach eggs and drain them well. Arrange on a platter, coat with soubise sauce and arrange the onion rings around them.

Eggs with Ham

(soft-cooked eggs)

8 eggs
$\frac{1}{2}$ lb package of macaroni
2 tablespoons butter
8 thin slices of cooked ham
3 tablespoons grated Swiss or Cheddar cheese
salt and pepper
2 cups béchamel sauce (made with 3 tablespoons butter, 3 tablespoons flour, 2 cups milk infused with slice of onion, bouquet garni, 6 peppercorns)

Method

Soft-cook the eggs and put in cold water.

Cook the macaroni in plenty of boiling salted water for 10–12 minutes or until tender. Drain, refresh under cold running water and return to the pan with 2 tablespoons butter. Reheat and spread in the bottom of a well-buttered gratin or baking dish. Keep hot.

Make the béchamel sauce.

Peel the eggs, wrap each in a slice of ham and arrange on the macaroni. Spoon over the béchamel sauce, sprinkle with grated cheese and brown lightly under the broiler or in a hot oven (400°F) for about 10 minutes.

Eggs Suzette

(soft-cooked or poached eggs)

4 eggs
4 Idaho potatoes
salt
1 cup ($\frac{1}{4}$ lb) sliced mushrooms
$\frac{1}{4}$ cup butter
2 teaspoons flour
$\frac{1}{4}$ cup stock
1 cup ($\frac{1}{4}$ lb) ham, cut in julienne strips
1 cup mornay sauce (made with $1\frac{1}{2}$ tablespoons butter, $1\frac{1}{2}$ tablespoons flour, 1 cup milk, and $\frac{1}{4}$ cup grated Swiss cheese)
3–4 tablespoons hot milk
$\frac{1}{4}$ cup grated Swiss or Cheddar cheese

Pastry bag and a large star tube (optional)

Method

Scrub potatoes, rub with salt, bake in moderate oven (350°F) for $1\frac{1}{4}$ hours or until tender.

Sauté mushrooms in 2 tablespoons of butter in a small pan. Stir in the flour, then the stock, bring to a boil and cook 1 minute. Add the ham, heat thoroughly, season to taste and set aside. Make mornay sauce. Soft cook or poach the eggs and keep in warm water.

Cut tops from potatoes (lengthwise) and scoop out pulp. Put into a warm bowl, mash and beat in 2 tablespoons butter and the hot milk to make a purée.

Put a quarter of the mushroom and ham mixture into the bottom of each potato, place a well drained egg on top and coat with mornay sauce. Top with potato purée, or fill a pastry bag fitted with a star tube and pipe potato to cover eggs completely. Sprinkle with grated cheese and brown under the broiler or in a hot oven (400°F) for about 10 minutes.

Eggs soubise are covered with an onion-flavored white sauce and decorated with fried onion rings

Eggs Mexicaine

(soft-cooked or poached eggs)

8 eggs
2 green bell peppers, cored and chopped
3 onions, finely chopped
6 tablespoons butter
1 large can (16 oz) corn kernels or 2 packages frozen corn kernels
2 tablespoons chili sauce
salt and pepper

For sauce
3 tablespoons butter
2 tablespoons flour
1½ cups milk
½ cup heavy cream
¾ cup grated Gruyère or Cheddar cheese

Method

Soft cook and peel, or poach, the eggs and put in cold water.

Blanch the peppers; sauté the onions in half the butter until brown and add peppers and corn, drained if canned or blanched if frozen. Add the remaining butter and the chili sauce. Season well and heat, shaking the pan occasionally until very hot. Reserve.

To make the sauce: melt the butter, stir in the flour off the heat and pour on the milk. Bring to a boil, stirring, and simmer 2 minutes. Take from the heat, stir in the cream and ½ cup cheese, a little at a time, and season to taste.

Spread the corn mixture in an ovenproof dish, arrange the eggs, well drained, on top and coat with the sauce. Sprinkle over the remaining ¼ cup cheese and brown under the broiler.

Eggs Benedict

(poached eggs)

8 eggs
8 thick slices of ham or Canadian bacon
2 tablespoons sherry or Madeira
4 English muffins
2 tablespoons butter
8 slices of truffle (optional)

For Hollandaise sauce
6 tablespoons white wine vinegar (seasoned with 6 peppercorns, blade of mace, slice of onion, and small bay leaf), or 1–2 tablespoons lemon juice
4 egg yolks
1 cup unsalted butter, slightly softened
salt and pepper
1–2 tablespoons light cream

Method

Cut circles from ham or bacon the same diameter as English muffins, pour sherry or Madeira over the slices, cover and warm on a heatproof plate in a very low oven (250°F).

To make Hollandaise sauce: in a small pan boil vinegar with its seasonings until reduced to a scant tablespoon. Set aside. With a wooden spoon, beat egg yolks in a bowl with ½ tablespoon butter and a pinch of salt until light and slightly thick. Strain on the vinegar or lemon juice, set bowl over a pan of boiling water, turn off heat and add remaining butter in small pieces, stirring vigorously.

Watchpoint: when adding butter, it should be slightly soft, not chilled.

When all butter has been added and sauce is thick, add cream and taste for seasoning. Sauce should be pleasantly sharp yet bland and have the consistency of heavy cream. Keep warm (not hot) in a water bath.

Poach the eggs and keep them in warm water.

Split and toast the English muffins and spread with butter. Lay a slice of ham or bacon on top of each muffin half and arrange on a hot platter. Drain the eggs, dry them thoroughly and place on top of the meat. Coat each egg with Hollandaise sauce and top with a slice of truffle, if you like. Serve at once.

Eggs en Surprise

(soft-cooked eggs)

6–8 small eggs

For soufflé mixture
1½ lb fresh or 2 packages frozen spinach
¼ cup butter
2 tablespoons flour
1 cup milk
pinch of grated nutmeg
salt and pepper
4 egg yolks
¾ cup chopped cooked ham (optional)
5 egg whites
2 tablespoons grated Parmesan cheese, mixed with 2 tablespoons browned breadcrumbs

6–8 individual cocottes or ramekins

Method

Soft cook the eggs; peel and put in cold water.

Wash the fresh spinach thoroughly and cook in boiling salted water for 5 minutes or until tender. Cook frozen spinach according to package directions. Drain, refresh under cold running water and press between 2 plates to dry thoroughly. Work the spinach through a sieve or purée it in a blender.

To make the soufflé mixture: melt 1 tablespoon butter in a pan, cook until nut-brown, then add the spinach purée and cook over medium heat, stirring, so that any excess liquid evaporates. Stir in the remaining butter, add flour and pour on the milk. Add nutmeg and season with salt and pepper to taste; bring mixture to a boil, stirring. Cool slightly and beat in the egg yolks, one at a time. Add the ham, if used.

Beat the egg whites until they hold a stiff peak and stir 2 tablespoons into the spinach mixture to soften it a little, then quickly fold in the remaining egg whites as lightly as possible. Butter the chosen dishes generously and put a layer of the soufflé mixture in the bottom of each one. Drain and dry the eggs and put one in each dish. Cover with remaining soufflé mixture, sprinkle tops with mixture of grated cheese and crumbs. Bake in a hot oven (400°F) for 10–12 minutes or until the soufflés are puffed. Serve at once.

Cocottes or ramekins

Many baked egg recipes may be cooked in individual cocottes or ramekins. Ramekins are small heatproof dishes shaped like miniature soufflé dishes. The sides of cocottes are not as straight and they often have handles (as shown in the photograph of convent eggs). If you have neither of these decorative dishes, use individual heatproof custard cups.

Convent Eggs
(baked eggs)

8 eggs
salt and pepper
$\frac{1}{2}$ cup heavy cream
3 tablespoons butter

8 individual cocottes or ramekins

This simple dish may be cooked in a large baking dish instead of in cocottes.

If you prefer, use tomato sauce instead of the cream and place some julienne strips of ham or chicken or slices of sautéed chicken liver in the cocottes under the eggs.

Method
Butter the dish or cocottes and sprinkle with salt and pepper. Break each egg into a cup and slide it carefully into the chosen dish. Pour 1 tablespoon cream over each egg. Set the dish or cocottes on a baking sheet and bake in a moderate oven (350°F) for 7–8 minutes or until the whites are almost firm and the yolk is barely set.

For convent eggs, butter individual cocottes before breaking in each egg ▸

Convent eggs are seasoned and covered with cream, then baked in individual dishes (recipe is on page 23)

Eggs Flamenco
(baked eggs)

8 eggs
6 tablespoons butter
3 potatoes, peeled, blanched and diced
3 frankfurters or any cooked smoked sausage, sliced
salt and pepper
3 tablespoons cooked peas
2 red bell peppers, cored, seeded and cut in strips, or 3 slices of canned pimiento, cut in strips
4 tomatoes, peeled, seeded and coarsely chopped
1 tablespoon chopped parsley
3 tablespoons light cream
$\frac{1}{4}$ teaspoon cayenne pepper

Method
Melt butter in a frying pan, add potatoes and sausages and cook over medium heat until potatoes start to brown, shaking pan occasionally to avoid sticking. Season, add peas and peppers and cook 5 minutes or until peppers are soft. Add tomatoes and parsley, cook until very hot and spread mixture in bottom of a buttered shallow ovenproof dish. Break the eggs on top, sprinkle with salt and pepper and pour over the cream. Bake in a moderate oven (350°F) for 8–10 minutes or until eggs are just set. Sprinkle with a very little cayenne pepper just before serving.

Root celery or celeriac looks like a large turnip or rutabaga. It tastes like regular celery and is good whether prepared on its own or added to beef and lamb stews. If possible choose small young roots as large ones can be quite tough. Peel celeriac before using.

Eggs Savoyarde
(baked eggs)

8 eggs
3 tablespoons butter
thick slice ($\frac{1}{4}$ lb) of uncooked ham, cut in strips
1 small root celery (celeriac), peeled and sliced
1 onion, sliced
3 medium potatoes, sliced
salt and pepper
6 tablespoons heavy cream
$\frac{1}{2}$ cup grated Gruyère cheese

Method
In a shallow saucepan melt butter and cook the ham for 1–2 minutes. Add the sliced vegetables, season, cover the pan with a tight-fitting lid and cook over low heat for 20 minutes or until the vegetables are tender but not browned.

Spread the ham mixture in a buttered ovenproof dish. Break the eggs on top, spoon over the cream and sprinkle with grated cheese. Bake in a moderate oven (350°F) for (8–10 minutes or until the eggs are just set.

Eggs à la Crème with Mushrooms
(baked eggs)

8 eggs
1 cup ($\frac{1}{4}$ lb) sliced mushrooms
squeeze of lemon juice
1 tablespoon butter
1 cup heavy cream
salt and pepper
pinch of grated nutmeg
1 cup grated Gruyère cheese

8 individual cocottes or ramekins

Method
Sauté mushrooms with lemon juice in butter for 3–4 minutes or until tender. Pour half the cream into the buttered dishes, then break the eggs on top carefully and cover with the mushrooms.

Season the remaining cream, add the nutmeg and spoon it over the mushrooms. Cover each dish with a thick layer of grated cheese, stand in a water bath of very hot water and bake in a moderate oven (350°F) for 10 minutes or until the eggs are lightly set.

Eggs Portugaise
(hard-cooked eggs)

8 eggs
3 tomatoes, peeled, seeded and sliced
6 tablespoons butter
$1\frac{1}{2}$ tablespoons mixed chopped herbs (parsley, chives, basil)
salt and pepper
$\frac{1}{2}$ cup grated Gruyère cheese

For sauce
2 tablespoons butter
2 tablespoons flour
$1\frac{1}{2}$ cups milk (infused with slice of onion, 1 carrot, sliced, bouquet garni, 6 peppercorns)
salt and pepper

Method
Hard cook the eggs and put in cold water. Sauté the tomatoes in 2 tablespoons of the butter for 1–2 minutes and arrange in an ovenproof dish.

Peel and cut the eggs in half lengthwise and scoop out the yolks. Work the yolks through a sieve; cream the remaining butter and mix it together with the egg yolks, chopped herbs, and salt and pepper to taste. Spoon the mixture into the egg whites and arrange them on the tomatoes.

To make the sauce: melt butter in a saucepan and stir in flour off the heat. Strain on the infused milk, return to the heat and bring to a boil, stirring constantly. Season with salt and pepper to taste and simmer 2–3 minutes.

Coat the eggs with the sauce, sprinkle with the grated cheese and bake in a hot oven (425°F) for 8–10 minutes or until brown.

Hungarian Eggs
(hard-cooked eggs)

8 eggs
4 medium onions, thinly sliced
2 tablespoons butter
2 large tomatoes, peeled, seeded and sliced
salt and pepper
$\frac{1}{2}$ teaspoon paprika
3–4 tablespoons tomato butter (for garnish)

Method
Hard cook the eggs and put in cold water. Sauté the onions in the butter until golden. Add tomatoes and cook 4–5 minutes or until the tomatoes are soft. Season to taste.

Peel and slice the eggs and arrange in an ovenproof dish, cover with the tomato mixture and sprinkle with paprika. Bake in a hot oven (425°F) for 7–8 minutes and garnish the top with circles of tomato butter.

Tomato Butter
Cream 3–4 tablespoons butter and work in $1\frac{1}{2}$ teaspoons tomato paste, 3–4 drops of Worcestershire sauce and salt and pepper. Roll into a cylinder the diameter of a half-dollar on wax paper and chill. Cut into circles.

Eggs à la Tripe
(hard-cooked eggs)

8 eggs
1 bunch of scallions or 2 medium onions
3 tablespoons butter
½ cup grated Gruyère or dry Cheddar cheese (for sprinkling)

For béchamel sauce
3 tablespoons butter
3 tablespoons flour
3 cups milk (infused with 6–8 sprigs of parsley, 6 peppercorns, blade of mace and 1 bay leaf)
salt and pepper

This dish takes its name from the egg whites that are cut in strips, resembling shreds of tripe.

Method
Hard cook eggs and put in cold water. Peel them, cut in half and scoop out the yolks. Wash the whites and cut into strips. Work the yolks through a sieve. Keep the whites and yolks in separate bowls covered with plastic wrap.

Cut scallions into 2–3 pieces or thinly slice regular onions. Blanch and drain them. Melt the 3 tablespoons butter in the pan, put in the scallions or onions, cover and cook very gently for 7–8 minutes or until tender but not brown; season well.

Make béchamel sauce. Butter an ovenproof dish and spread the egg whites over the bottom. Scatter on the scallions or onions and lastly the sieved egg yolks. Spoon the sauce over the top, sprinkle with grated cheese and bake in a hot oven (400°F) for 7–10 minutes or until brown.

Eggs Cantalienne
(hard-cooked eggs)

8 eggs
1 medium head of green cabbage
6 tablespoons butter
¾ cup white wine or stock
salt and pepper
3 shallots, finely chopped
½ cup browned breadcrumbs

For sauce
3 tablespoons butter
2 tablespoons flour
1½ cups milk
1 teaspoon Dijon-style mustard
½ cup grated Cantal or Cheddar cheese

Cantal is a cheese from the Auvergne district of France; it is made from a mixture of cow's, ewe's and goat's milk. Cheddar cheese is a good substitute.

Method
Hard cook the eggs and put in cold water. Shred the cabbage finely, discarding the hard core, and blanch it in boiling salted water for 1 minute; drain. In a pan melt 3 tablespoons of the butter and add the cabbage with the wine or stock. Season, cover with buttered foil and the lid and cook 5–6 minutes or until the cabbage is just tender.

To make the sauce: in a saucepan melt butter, stir in flour off the heat and pour on half the milk. Bring the mixture to a boil, stirring, and simmer 2 minutes. Take from the heat and stir in the mustard with the cheese, reserving 2 tablespoons; then season to taste.

Melt the remaining 3 tablespoons butter and cook the shallots slowly until soft.

Peel and split the eggs lengthwise, scoop out the yolks and work them through a sieve. Mix them with the shallots and 2 tablespoons of the sauce and season to taste. Fill the whites with the mixture. Add remaining milk to the sauce and reheat.

Arrange the cabbage down the center of a heated platter, place the eggs on top and spoon over the sauce. Sprinkle with browned breadcrumbs, mixed with the remaining 2 tablespoons cheese, and brown under the broiler or in a hot oven (400°F) for about 10 minutes.

Eggs Romaine
(fried eggs)

8 eggs
1½ lb fresh or 2 packages frozen spinach
3 tablespoons butter
deep fat or oil (for frying)
salt and pepper
6 anchovy fillets, or 2–3 slices of bacon (for garnish)

For light cream sauce
1 cup light cream
squeeze of lemon juice

Method
Wash fresh spinach thoroughly and cook 4–5 minutes in boiling salted water or until just tender. Cook frozen spinach according to package directions. Drain well and chop finely or leave whole 'en branche'.

Wipe out pan, cook butter in it to a nut-brown, add spinach and cook it quickly to evaporate any moisture. Fry eggs in deep fat, drain and sprinkle them with salt and pepper.

Arrange the spinach on a hot platter and place the eggs on top. Garnish with the anchovy fillets, split in two lengthwise, or with crisply fried slices of bacon.

To make the sauce: heat the light cream with salt, pepper and a squeeze of lemon juice and serve separately.

Eggs Gascon
(fried eggs)

4–8 eggs
1 eggplant, sliced
1 large onion, thinly sliced
¾ cup oil
3 tomatoes, peeled and thickly sliced
salt and pepper
1 thick slice of uncooked ham, cut in strips

Method
Sprinkle the eggplant slices with salt, leave 30 minutes, then rinse in cold water to remove the salt (this process, called 'dégorger', draws out the bitter juices of the eggplant).

Sauté onion in 2 tablespoons oil until brown, remove and set aside. Dry eggplant slices on paper towels, add 6 tablespoons oil to pan and fry eggplant until golden brown on both sides. Pour away any excess fat and add tomatoes and onion. Season and cook 6–7 minutes or until mixture is rich and pulpy. Spoon into a hot serving dish and keep warm.

Wipe out the pan, heat the remaining oil and fry the ham for 3–4 minutes or until brown; drain and reserve. Fry the eggs in the same pan and place on top of the eggplant mixture. Scatter the ham on top and serve at once.

Eggs gascon is a substantial dish of fried eggs with strips of ham, sliced eggplant, onion and tomato. Serve it very hot

The ingredients for eggs Xérès, an unusual dish that is named for the sherry in which the carrots are cooked

Scrambled Eggs Xérès

8 eggs
3 medium carrots
½ cup butter
6 tablespoons sherry
salt and pepper
grated rind of 1 orange
juice of ½ orange
3 tablespoons heavy cream
bunch of watercress (for garnish) – optional

Xérès is the ancient name for Jerez in Spain, the home of sherry.

Method

Peel carrots, slice thinly lengthwise, then cut across into julienne strips.

Melt 2 tablespoons butter in a small pan, add the carrots and cook gently for 2–3 minutes. Add the sherry, season, cover tightly and cook 5 minutes or until the carrots are tender and the sherry has almost been absorbed. Take from the heat and add the grated orange rind and juice.

Break the eggs into a bowl, beat with a fork until frothy, season and add the cream. Stir in the carrot mixture. In a fairly large pan melt the remaining butter, pour in the egg mixture and cook, stirring, over very low heat. When thickened to your taste, spoon into a hot dish, garnish with watercress and serve at once.

Scrambled Eggs with Asparagus

8 eggs
1–1½ lb fresh or 1 package frozen asparagus
salt and pepper
½ cup butter
1 cup yogurt or sour cream

For croûtons
4–6 slices of stale bread, diced, with crusts removed
2 tablespoons butter

Method

Cook fresh asparagus in boiling salted water for 8–10 minutes or until just tender, or cook frozen asparagus according to the package directions. Drain thoroughly and keep warm.

Break eggs into a bowl, beat with a fork to mix and season with salt and pepper.

To make croûtons: heat butter in a skillet and fry the bread, turning so the croûtons brown evenly. Drain and reserve.

Melt 3 tablespoons butter in a heavy-based pan, add about two-thirds of the egg mixture and cook over very low heat, stirring, until thick and creamy. Add the remaining eggs with the cream and the rest of the butter and continue stirring over heat until very thick. Pile in a hot dish and surround with fried croûtons and asparagus.

Garlic Butter

Cream ¼ cup butter and beat in 2 cloves of garlic (or to taste) crushed with ¼ teaspoon salt. Season with plenty of freshly ground black pepper.

Pipérade
(scrambled eggs)

8 eggs
3 red bell peppers, cored, seeded and chopped
3 ripe tomatoes, peeled, seeded and coarsely chopped
6 tablespoons butter
2 shallots, finely chopped
3 cloves of garlic, finely chopped
salt and pepper
8–10 slices of bread, cut in 1½ inch rounds (for croûtes)
¼ cup garlic butter

This dish, from the Basque region of the Pyrenees, is a mixture of sweet red peppers, tomatoes and eggs, well flavored with garlic. It can be eaten hot or cold.

Method

Blanch peppers in boiling salted water for 2 minutes and drain.

Melt half the butter in a skillet, add the tomatoes, peppers, shallots and garlic. Season well and cook over low heat, stirring occasionally, until mixture is a thick pulp.

Break the eggs into a bowl and beat with a fork to mix. Spread the rounds of bread with a little garlic butter on both sides and bake in a moderate oven (350°F) for 10–12 minutes or until crisp.

Add remaining butter with eggs to mixture in the skillet and cook over low heat, stirring with a metal spoon, until eggs start to thicken creamily. Spoon into a hot dish and surround with croûtes.

For a picnic, cut the top from a small loaf of French bread and scoop out most of the crumb. Spread inside of the loaf and the lid with garlic butter and bake in a moderate oven (350°F) for 15–18 minutes or until lightly crisp. Fill with the pipérade and replace the lid. When cold, cut in slices and serve.

Scotch Woodcock
(scrambled eggs)

8 eggs
12–16 anchovy fillets, soaked in 3 tablespoons milk
4 slices of bread
½ cup butter, softened
pepper

This dish is a typical British 'savory', served instead of dessert to end a meal. The egg should not be smooth, but cooked to large, creamy flakes.

Method

Drain the anchovy fillets and pound with a mortar and pestle until smooth, or chop finely.

Toast the bread, remove the crusts, spread with 2 tablespoons butter (reserving 6 tablespoons) and arrange on a warm platter. In a bowl beat the eggs with a fork to mix. Add the anchovy, pepper to taste and half the reserved butter in small pieces. Melt remaining butter in a skillet or frying pan, add the egg and anchovy mixture and cook over low heat, stirring, until it begins to thicken. Then with a metal spatula lift big flakes of lightly cooked scrambled egg mixture from the bottom of the pan, continuing until it is lightly cooked, or firm, to your taste. Spoon onto the toast and serve at once.

COLD EGG DISHES

Eggs Mollets à l'Indienne

(soft-cooked or poached eggs)

8 eggs
$\frac{3}{4}$ cup rice, cooked, drained and dried
$\frac{1}{4}$ cup vinaigrette dressing
1 cup mayonnaise
salt and pepper

For curry mixture
1 shallot, finely chopped
1$\frac{1}{2}$ tablespoons oil
1 tablespoon curry powder
1$\frac{1}{2}$ teaspoons paprika
$\frac{3}{4}$ cup tomato juice
3 slices of lemon
1 tablespoon apricot jam

For garnish
slice of pimiento, cut in strips
bunch of watercress

Method

To make the curry mixture: sauté shallot in oil until soft, add the curry powder and paprika and cook, stirring, for 4–5 seconds. Add the remaining ingredients, stir well and simmer 4–5 minutes. Strain and reserve.

Soft cook or poach the eggs and keep in cold water. Toss the rice and vinaigrette dressing with a fork and arrange down the center of a platter. Drain the eggs well and arrange on top of the rice. Add enough of the curry mixture to the mayonnaise to flavor it well and thin it to a coating consistency. Adjust the seasoning and spoon the curry mayonnaise over the eggs. Garnish with strips of pimiento and watercress.

A l'Indienne (in Indian style) usually refers to dishes that contain either curry or chutney or both, accompanied by a dish of plain boiled rice.

To dry boiled rice: after draining, turn it onto a large platter and leave in a very low oven to dry for at least 15 minutes before use or serving.

Anchovy Eggs

(hard-cooked eggs)

8 eggs
12–16 anchovy fillets, soaked in 3 tablespoons milk
6 tablespoons butter
black pepper, freshly ground
1 cup mayonnaise
1 tablespoon chopped mixed herbs (parsley, thyme, basil) – optional
bunch of watercress (for garnish)

Method

Hard cook the eggs, peel and cut in half lengthwise. Drain anchovy fillets and pound until smooth. Scoop the yolks from the egg whites and work them with the butter into the anchovies. Season with black pepper, put into the whites and sandwich the halves together again.

Thin the mayonnaise to a coating consistency, if necessary, add the herbs, if used, and spoon over the eggs. Garnish with sprigs of watercress.

Eggs Mikado

(poached eggs)

8 eggs
$\frac{3}{4}$ cup rice, cooked, drained and dried
3 slices of canned pimiento, cut in strips
3–4 stalks of celery, thinly sliced
$\frac{1}{4}$ cup vinaigrette dressing
1 cup mayonnaise
1 hard-cooked egg
1$\frac{1}{2}$ tablespoons chopped parsley
1 teaspoon chopped chives (optional)
watercress (for garnish) – optional

Method

Poach the eggs and put in cold water.

Add pimiento, celery and vinaigrette dressing to the rice, stir with a fork and spoon mixture down the center of a platter. Drain and dry poached eggs and set them on the rice.

If necessary, thin mayonnaise to a coating consistency with a little hot water; spoon a little over eggs so they are coated but the salad can still be seen.

Peel the hard-cooked egg, take out yolk and press it through a sieve over platter so the yolk is sprinkled all over the dish. Scatter with chopped parsley and chives and garnish with watercress if you like.

Note: leftover white of hard-cooked egg may be cut in strips and added to the rice salad with the pimiento and celery.

Vinaigrette Dressing

For $\frac{1}{2}$ cup: mix 2 tablespoons vinegar (any of the following types: red or white wine, cider or tarragon) with $\frac{1}{2}$ teaspoon salt and $\frac{1}{2}$ teaspoon freshly ground black pepper. Gradually add 6 tablespoons olive or peanut oil, whisking until dressing thickens slightly. Taste for seasoning. Chopped fresh herbs (thyme, marjoram, basil or parsley) are an excellent addition, as is a pinch of sugar, according to your taste.

Eggs mollets à l'Indienne are garnished with strips of pimiento

For eggs mimosa the remaining yolks are sieved over the filled eggs; garnish with watercress

For eggs mimosa, sieve half the egg yolks and mix with the coarsely chopped shrimps

Bind the yolk and shrimp mixture with thick mayonnaise for eggs mimosa

Eggs Mimosa
(hard-cooked eggs)

4–6 large eggs
$\frac{1}{2}$ lb peeled cooked shrimps, coarsely chopped
1$\frac{1}{2}$ cups thick mayonnaise
bunch of watercress (for garnish)
buttered wholewheat bread (for serving)

The egg yolk garnish for eggs mimosa has the same fluffy texture and bright yellow color as a mimosa blossom.

Method

Hard cook the eggs, peel and split them lengthwise. Scoop out the yolks and carefully work half of them through a sieve into a bowl. Add the shrimps and bind the mixture with 2–3 tablespoons mayonnaise.

Rinse the egg whites, dry them and arrange on a platter. Fill them with the shrimp mixture. Thin the remaining mayonnaise slightly with a little hot water and coat the eggs with this. Hold the sieve over the eggs and work the remaining egg yolks through so each egg is sprinkled with yolk. Garnish the dish with watercress and serve with buttered wholewheat bread.

Oeufs en Gelée Simple
(Quick soft-cooked Eggs in Aspic)

4 small eggs
2 cans consomme
1 envelope gelatin
2 tablespoons brandy or sherry
2 thin slices of ham
4 slices of truffle or 1 small mushroom, thinly sliced
squeeze of lemon juice (optional)
bunch of watercress (for garnish)

4 oval eggs-in-aspic, or dariole, molds (2–2$\frac{1}{2}$ inches deep)

These are soft-cooked eggs set in special individual molds designed to hold 1 egg each, with aspic and garnish. A more elaborate version, using home-made aspic, will be given in a future Volume.

Method

Sprinkle the gelatin over $\frac{1}{2}$ can of the consommé, let stand 5 minutes until spongy and dissolve over gentle heat. Stir the gelatin mixture with the brandy or sherry into the remaining consommé.

Soft cook the eggs, cool, peel and keep in cold water. Cut ovals of ham slightly smaller than the bottom of the molds.

Watchpoint: if the ham ovals are too large, they will stick to the sides of the molds and remain in them when the eggs are turned out.

If using the mushrooms, in a small saucepan cook them with the lemon juice in 1–2 tablespoons water for 1–2 minutes or until tender. Drain.

Set the molds in a roasting pan of ice water and add a thin layer of cool but still liquid aspic to each mold. When cold and set, arrange a piece of truffle or a slice of mushroom on top, add 1 tablespoon more of cool but still liquid aspic and chill again until set. Add the ovals of ham.

Drain the eggs thoroughly on paper towels and set them on top of the ham; half fill the mold with more cool but still liquid aspic. Leave until set, then fill the molds with the remaining aspic, so the eggs are thoroughly covered. Chill in the refrigerator at least 2 hours or until firmly set.

A short time before serving, turn out the molds and garnish each plate with a few sprigs of watercress.

To Turn Out Small Molds

Have ready a bowl of hand-hot water, a sheet of wax paper dampened with cold water, a metal spatula and a prepared platter.

Grip the mold firmly with the palm of your hand over the top and gently swish it through the hot water once or twice.

Still holding the mold, turn it over so your palm is underneath and the mold on top. Sharply knock the mold with the fingers of your other hand until the contents drop onto your open palm. Slide the mold gently onto the dampened wax paper before transferring it to the platter with the metal spatula.

Eggs with Tuna
(hard-cooked eggs)

8 eggs
1 can $3\frac{1}{4}$ oz tuna, flaked
6 tablespoons butter, softened, or $\frac{1}{4}$ cup mayonnaise
salt and pepper

For béchamel sauce
2 tablespoons butter
2 tablespoons flour
1 cup milk (infused with 1 bay leaf, slice of onion, blade of mace and 6 peppercorns)

For salad
$\frac{1}{2}$ lb green beans, cooked
1 cup ripe olives, pitted
6 medium tomatoes, peeled, seeded and quartered
$\frac{1}{2}$ cup vinaigrette dressing (see page 30), lightly flavored with garlic

Pastry bag and a $\frac{3}{8}$ inch plain tube

Meat, chicken, ham or other fish can be used instead of the tuna.

Method
Hard cook eggs and put in cold water. Make the béchamel sauce, cover and cool.

Peel and halve the eggs and scoop out the yolks. Sieve the yolks into a bowl and pound them with the tuna, béchamel sauce and the softened butter or mayonnaise. Season well.

Rinse and dry the whites and arrange them around a platter, securing with a little of the tuna mixture. Fill the remainder into a pastry bag fitted with a $\frac{3}{8}$ inch plain tube and pipe into the whites. Toss the ingredients for the salad with the vinaigrette dressing and pile in the center of the dish.

Omelets

Any lesson on eggs would be incomplete without some omelets, although savory omelets were covered in Volume 1 and soufflé omelets will be discussed in a future Volume. The following three recipes are fairly substantial variations on the omelet theme; they are not folded in the French manner, but served flat and often cut into wedges.

Omelet Arnold Bennett

8 eggs, separated
$\frac{1}{2}$ cup cooked Finnan haddie, flaked
6 tablespoons butter
1 cup heavy cream
salt and pepper
5 tablespoons grated Parmesan cheese

This is an elegant dish created by the Savoy Grill in London in honor of the writer, Arnold Bennett.

Method
In a saucepan melt 3 tablespoons of the butter, add the haddock with $\frac{1}{4}$ cup cream and stir over high heat for 2–3 minutes. Cool.

Beat the egg yolks with 2 tablespoons cream. Beat the egg whites until they hold a soft peak and fold into the yolks with the haddock and half the cheese. Season.

Melt the remaining butter in an omelet pan or skillet and cook the omelet. Do not fold, but slide onto a warm heatproof serving dish. Sprinkle on the rest of the cheese, pour over the remaining cream and brown quickly under a hot broiler. Serve at once.

Spanish Omelet 1

8 eggs, well beaten
7 tablespoons olive oil
$\frac{1}{2}$ cup ($\frac{1}{4}$ lb) chopped raw ham
1 large Bermuda onion, sliced
1 clove of garlic, crushed (optional)
2 medium potatoes, peeled and sliced or coarsely grated
salt and pepper

A true Spanish omelet is made with a base of potatoes and onion, cooked in olive oil and flavored with garlic. Another version that includes cooked mixed vegetables is a good way of using leftovers. The consistency of both omelets should be firm but not too solid. To serve, cut into wedges, like a cake.

Method
Heat the oil in a frying pan or skillet, add the chopped ham and fry until it starts to brown. Add the onion and the crushed garlic, if you like. Fry until the onion is soft, then add the potato. Season well and cook until the potato is tender.

Drain off any extra fat and pour the beaten eggs into the pan. Stir to mix, then cook until the bottom of the omelet is brown. Loosen the omelet with a metal spatula. The top of the mixture will be hardly set, so put the pan under the broiler for a few moments to brown the surface. Turn out the omelet onto a flat platter, cut into wedges and serve with peperoni.

Spanish Omelet 2

8 eggs, well beaten
6 tablespoons olive oil
2 cloves of garlic
2 cups cooked mixed vegetables (e.g. carrots, potatoes, peas, sweet red pepper), diced
2 tomatoes, peeled, seeded and sliced
salt and pepper

Method
In a large skillet heat the oil and fry the garlic gently for 1 minute. Remove it and discard. Add the mixed vegetables and tomatoes and cook until very hot, shaking the pan to prevent the mixture from sticking.

Pour beaten eggs into the pan and season. Stir to mix, then leave on low heat until the eggs are set.

Loosen the omelet with a metal spatula, then brown the surface, under the broiler. Slide onto a flat platter and cut into wedges to serve.

Peperoni

2 green bell peppers, cored, seeded and thinly sliced
2 red bell peppers, cored, seeded and thinly sliced
2 tablespoons butter
1 medium onion, sliced
1 clove of garlic, crushed
salt and pepper

Method
If you prefer, blanch the peppers to tone down their flavor. Melt the butter in a pan, add the onion and the crushed garlic and cook slowly until soft but not browned. Add the peppers with salt and pepper to taste and cook until just tender.

Spanish omelet 1 is made with chopped ham and potatoes. Cut it into wedges and serve with peperoni

COOK'S VACATION

When you want to take a rest from cooking and simplify your menus, choose foods that are cooked together in one big casserole – this reduces the preparations and dish washing. Casserole dishes reheat so well that you can make a double quantity and serve the leftovers another day. Make use of convenience foods to save time and energy, and keep a regular stock of fruit, cheese, cookies and snacks to satisfy hearty appetites.

Basic Equipment

Good food does not depend on the number of pots and pans you use.

The most important item is the stove, but remarkably good meals can be prepared in an electric skillet or on a single burner.

Two pans are indispensable: a large enameled cast iron casserole or Dutch oven, and a heavy frying pan or skillet, with a lid. To these two you can add a small saucepan, a kettle and an asbestos mat. You'll need one good sharp knife, a small vegetable knife and a slotted metal spatula for frying. Add a couple of bowls, a large strainer to double as a colander, a carving board that can be used for chopping, and your basic equipment is complete.

Note: when reheating cooked dishes, reheat quickly and thoroughly at medium heat for 10–15 minutes.

Foods for the Cupboard

Stock up with some of the following canned/dried foods.

Salt and pepper; mustard and tomato paste; mayonnaise and salad dressing; curry powder; ketchup; pickles.

Dried and evaporated milk; tea; instant coffee; cocoa; soft drinks.

Rice; spaghetti or macaroni; jam; honey; maple syrup; crackers; cookies; chocolate bars.

Canned soups such as tomato, mushroom, celery, consommé (to use in stews), vegetable beef.

Cans of ham and corned beef; sardines; salmon; tuna; baked beans; canned fruit and vegetable juices; tomatoes (for mixing with stews and casseroles); corn kernels; sauerkraut (to serve with ham or frankfurters); pineapple; peaches; pears.

Dried or dehydrated foods: rice pilaf packages; mixed vegetables; instant mashed potatoes; soups; white sauce; peas and other vegetables.

Cans for special occasions: liver pâté; crab meat; shrimps; chicken breasts; artichoke bottoms; lychees; figs.

Egg and Tuna Cream

1 large can ($9\frac{1}{4}$ oz) tuna in water or oil
6 hard-cooked eggs, quartered or sliced
1 tablespoon browned breadcrumbs
1 tablespoon grated cheese

For sauce
$\frac{1}{4}$ cup butter
2 medium onions, thinly sliced
2 tablespoons flour
2 cups milk
salt and pepper
6 tablespoons grated Swiss or Cheddar cheese

Method

To make the sauce: melt half the butter, add onion and cook until soft. Add remaining butter and, when melted, stir in the flour. Pour on the milk, bring to a boil, stirring, and simmer 2 minutes. Take from the heat and gradually beat in the 6 tablespoons cheese; taste for seasoning.

Pour a little sauce into a baking dish, drain and flake the tuna and arrange in the dish with hard-cooked eggs on top. Coat with remaining sauce. Sprinkle the browned breadcrumbs mixed with the cheese on top and bake in a moderately hot oven (375°F) for 20–25 minutes or until the dish is well browned.

If you like, the dish can be prepared earlier in the day and baked just before serving.

Fish Monte Carlo

$1\frac{1}{2}$ lb cooked white fish – haddock, flounder, cod, etc.
3 tablespoons butter
3 tablespoons flour
2 cups milk
pinch of dry mustard
salt and pepper
1 medium can (1 lb) corn kernels, drained
2 eggs, separated
6 tablespoons grated Swiss or Cheddar cheese
2 tablespoons browned breadcrumbs

For serving
6–8 slices of bacon, crisply fried
$1\frac{1}{2}$ cups tomato sauce

Method

Flake fish, removing any skin and bones. Melt the butter, stir in flour and pour in milk. Bring to a boil, stirring, add mustard with salt and pepper to taste and simmer 2 minutes. Take from the heat and stir in the corn. Beat in egg yolks and cheese, reserving 2 tablespoons for the top.

Whip the egg whites until they hold a stiff peak and fold into the sauce.

Butter a baking dish and fill with alternating layers of fish and sauce, finishing with sauce. Sprinkle the reserved cheese mixed with the breadcrumbs on top and bake in a moderate oven (350°F) for 25–30 minutes or until very hot and brown.

If you like, the dish can be prepared earlier in the day and baked just before serving.

Garnish with the bacon and serve tomato sauce separately.

Clam Casserole

$1\frac{1}{2}$ cups shucked, chopped clams, or 2 cans ($7\frac{1}{2}$ oz each) minced clams, drained
$\frac{3}{4}$ cup butter
2 onions, finely sliced
2 green bell peppers, cored and cut in strips
3 cups crushed unsalted crackers
1 teaspoon thyme
1 tablespoon chopped parsley
salt and pepper

Method

In a skillet melt $\frac{1}{4}$ cup butter and fry onions until soft. Add green peppers and cook until soft. Stir in the remaining butter until melted. Put a layer of crumbs in a casserole, and spoon over some of the onion, pepper and butter mixture. Then spread with a layer of clams and moisten with any clam juice. Sprinkle with herbs and salt and pepper to taste. Continue adding ingredients in layers until all are used, ending with cracker crumbs, moistened with the remaining melted butter.

Bake the casserole in a moderate oven (350°F) for 25–30 minutes or until brown.

If you like, prepare the dish earlier in the day and bake just before serving.

Note: when reheating cooked dishes, reheat quickly and thoroughly at medium heat for 10–15 minutes.

Sardines with Tomatoes

2–3 cans sardines in oil
salt and pepper
3 tablespoons olive oil
3 tablespoons chopped mixed herbs (parsley, chives, dill, basil)
3 tablespoons chopped capers or gherkin pickles
4–5 tomatoes, peeled
3 tablespoons browned breadcrumbs, or grated Parmesan cheese

Method

Set oven at moderate (350°F).

Drain the sardines and, if you like, remove the skin and backbones. Lay them in a baking dish and sprinkle with salt and pepper and a little of the oil. Scatter over the herbs and capers or gherkin pickles.

Cut the tomatoes in thick slices and lay in the baking dish on top of the sardines. Sprinkle over remaining oil and scatter with crumbs or, if you like, grated Parmesan cheese. Bake in heated oven for 20–30 minutes or until very hot.

This dish is good served hot or cold. If served cold, omit the breadcrumbs or grated cheese.

Tuna with Tomatoes

Make as for sardines with tomatoes, but use 1 large can ($9\frac{1}{4}$ oz) of tuna instead of the sardines.

Pigs in a Blanket

1 package unbaked flaky crescent rolls
12 small frankfurters
2–3 teaspoons prepared mustard
$\frac{1}{4}$ cup finely chopped sweet relish
1 egg, beaten to mix

Method

Unwrap the sheet of dough for the rolls, keeping it in one piece. Roll it out to a 9 X 12 inch rectangle and cut it into 3 inch squares. On each square put a frankfurter, add a little mustard and 1 teaspoon of relish and roll up.

Brush the rolls with beaten egg, place on a cookie sheet and bake in a hot oven (400°F) for 10–12 minutes or until brown. Serve hot or cold.

Quick Chicken Tetrazzini

3–$3\frac{1}{2}$ lb roasting chicken, cooked
$\frac{1}{2}$–$\frac{3}{4}$ lb egg noodles
1 can (4 oz) sliced mushrooms, drained
$\frac{1}{4}$ cup grated Parmesan cheese

For sauce
3 tablespoons butter
3 tablespoons flour
2 cups chicken stock
pinch of nutmeg
salt and pepper
1 cup light cream or milk
2 tablespoons sherry (optional)

Method

Cut the chicken meat from the bones. If you like, make stock from these bones; otherwise use canned or powdered chicken stock.

To make the sauce: melt butter in a saucepan, stir in flour and pour on the stock. Bring sauce to a boil, stirring, season with the nutmeg and salt and pepper to taste and simmer 2 minutes. Stir in the cream or milk and sherry.

Cook the noodles in plenty of boiling salted water for 8–10 minutes or until just tender. Drain them and rinse under hot water to remove the starch.

Lay half the noodles in the bottom of a casserole or baking dish, cover with half the chicken and spoon over half the sauce. Add the remaining noodles, then the chicken and cover with the drained mushrooms. Coat with remaining sauce and sprinkle with Parmesan cheese. Bake in a moderate oven (350°F) for 25–30 minutes or until brown.

If you like, prepare the casserole earlier in the day and bake just before serving.

Mock Puchero

4–6 pieces of chicken
$\frac{1}{4}$ cup oil
$\frac{1}{2}$ lb country sausages
1 cup canned tomatoes
1 can (1 lb) baked beans in tomato sauce
$\frac{3}{4}$ cup rice
$\frac{1}{2}$ cup chicken stock
salt and pepper

Method

Heat oil in a flameproof casserole and cook the sausages over medium heat until brown. Take out and cut in thick diagonal slices. Add the chicken to the casserole and fry 10 minutes, browning on all sides. Take out, pour off all but 2 tablespoons fat, then return the ingredients to the pot in this order: chicken pieces, slices of sausage, tomatoes, baked

Mock puchero can be cooked on top of the stove or in the oven

beans, rice and stock.

Add salt and pepper to taste, cover casserole and simmer on top of the stove for about 30 minutes, or bake in a moderate oven (350°F) for 35–45 minutes or until the chicken is tender and the rice is cooked. This casserole reheats well.

Fry sausages until they are brown and cut them into thick diagonal slices for puchero

Layer the puchero ingredients in a flameproof casserole for the final cooking

Quick goulash is garnished with a border of finely chopped parsley and served with boiled rice

Quick Goulash

$1\frac{1}{2}$–2 lb round or chuck steak
2 tablespoons oil or butter
1 tablespoon paprika
1 tablespoon dried onion flakes
1 can tomato soup, diluted as directed on can
salt and pepper
$\frac{1}{2}$ cup plain yogurt or sour cream
2 tablespoons chopped parsley (for garnish)

Method

Cut meat into $1\frac{1}{2}$ inch squares and brown in oil in a flameproof casserole. Stir in the paprika and cook gently for 1 minute. Add onion and tomato soup, cover tightly and simmer gently on top of the stove or bake in a moderate oven (350°F) for $1\frac{1}{2}$–2 hours or until the meat is tender.

Just before serving, taste for seasoning and stir in the yogurt or sour cream. Scatter over the chopped parsley to form a border around the edge. Serve with boiled rice.

Note: when reheating cooked dishes, reheat quickly and thoroughly at medium heat for 10–15 minutes.

Smothered Beef Casserole

3 lb round steak or rolled rump of beef, with some fat
$\frac{1}{4}$ lb salt pork or bacon, sliced
pinch of cinnamon
pinch of allspice
salt and pepper
2 onions, quartered
3–4 carrots, quartered
1 clove of garlic, crushed
2 cups red wine
about 2 cups water
3–4 medium potatoes, peeled and quartered

Method

In a large flameproof casserole, place pork or bacon and set beef on top. Add the spices with salt and pepper to taste and put vegetables around the meat. Add garlic with wine and enough water almost to cover the meat. Cover tightly with the lid and cook just below simmering point over very low heat on top of the stove or in a low oven (300°F) for 3–4 hours, or until the meat is very tender and the gravy is reduced by half. Add the potatoes 20 minutes before the end of cooking.

This dish reheats well. If reheating do not cook potatoes completely during first cooking.

Pastitso

$\frac{1}{2}$ lb macaroni
3 tablespoons olive oil
2 onions, sliced
1 lb ground beef
$1\frac{1}{2}$ cups canned tomatoes
$\frac{1}{2}$ teaspoon allspice
$\frac{1}{2}$ teaspoon thyme
$\frac{1}{2}$ teaspoon rosemary
salt and pepper
2 eggs
2 cups milk
$\frac{1}{2}$ cup grated Swiss cheese

Method

In a skillet heat oil and fry onions until soft. Add beef and cook until brown, stirring. Add tomatoes, allspice, herbs and salt and pepper to taste and simmer 10 minutes.

Cook macaroni in plenty of boiling salted water for 10–12 minutes or until just tender. Drain and rinse with hot water to remove the starch.

Butter a baking dish and put a layer of macaroni, then a layer of beef mixture into it; continue until both are used, ending with macaroni. Beat the eggs with the milk until thoroughly mixed, add a little salt and pepper and pour into the baking dish. Sprinkle with the cheese and bake in a moderate oven (350°F) for 45 minutes or until firm and golden. Cool a little before cutting into squares to serve.

Stuffed Baked Potatoes

4 very large or 6 medium Idaho or baking potatoes
1 tablespoon oil
2 onions, chopped
1 lb ground beef
1 cup ($\frac{1}{4}$ lb) chopped mushrooms, or 1 can (4 oz) chopped mushrooms, drained
2 tablespoons chopped parsley
1 teaspoon chopped thyme
1 teaspoon chili pepper
salt and pepper
$\frac{1}{4}$ cup grated Swiss or Cheddar cheese

Method

Wash the potatoes, rub them with salt, prick with a fork and bake in a moderate oven (350°F) for 1 hour or until very soft. Cut them in half lengthwise, scoop out the pulp and mash it.

In a skillet heat the oil, add the onions and fry until brown. Stir in the ground beef and cook over moderate heat until brown. Stir in the mushrooms, parsley, thyme, chili pepper, and salt and pepper to taste and cook 1 minute longer. Take from the heat, mix in the potato pulp and spoon the mixture back into the potato shells.

Scatter the tops with grated cheese and bake in a moderate oven (350°F) for 20 minutes or until heated through and browned.

The potatoes may be prepared earlier in the day and heated just before serving.

DESSERTS

Banana Coconut Rolls
with Rum or Pineapple Sauce

6 bananas, peeled
2 tablespoons melted butter
juice of 1 lemon
$\frac{1}{2}$ cup shredded coconut

Method
Set oven at moderately hot (375°F).

Brush the bananas (they should be firm and not too ripe) with melted butter and sprinkle with lemon juice. Halve them crosswise, place in a buttered baking dish and sprinkle with coconut.

Bake in heated oven for 15–20 minutes or until the bananas are tender and the coconut is browned. Serve hot or cold with rum or pineapple sauce.

Rum Sauce

Dissolve $\frac{1}{2}$ cup sugar in $\frac{1}{2}$ cup hot water, bring to a boil and boil 5 minutes. Take from heat and add 2 tablespoons dark rum, or to taste, and 1 teaspoon lime juice.

Pineapple Sauce

Mix 2 tablespoons sugar, 2 teaspoons cornstarch and a pinch of salt together. Stir in $\frac{3}{4}$ cup unsweetened pineapple juice, bring to a boil, stirring, and simmer 2 minutes. Add 1 teaspoon lemon juice and $\frac{3}{4}$ cup fresh or canned crushed pineapple.

Quick Chocolate Fudge Cake

2 squares (2 oz) sweet chocolate
$\frac{1}{3}$ cup butter
1 cup sugar
2 eggs, beaten to mix
$\frac{1}{2}$ teaspoon vanilla
$\frac{3}{4}$ cup flour
$\frac{3}{4}$ cup coarsely chopped pecans or walnuts
1 cup heavy cream, stiffly whipped (for serving) – optional

8 inch square cake pan

Method
Set oven at moderately hot (375°F) and grease pan.

In a saucepan melt butter with chocolate over gentle heat. Take from heat; stir in sugar, eggs, vanilla, flour and pecans or walnuts. Pour into greased pan; bake in heated oven for 25 minutes or until cake shrinks from sides of pan. Cool for 5 minutes, turn out onto a wire rack and cool completely. If you like, spread with stiffly whipped cream before serving.

Peach Cream Pie

$1\frac{1}{2}$ cup quantity of pie pastry (see Volume 1)

For filling
5 fresh peaches, peeled or canned peaches, drained
1 package (8 oz) cream cheese
$\frac{1}{2}$ cup sugar
2 eggs
$\frac{1}{2}$ teaspoon cinnamon
$\frac{1}{4}$ cup peach preserves

9 inch pie pan

Method
Roll out the pastry dough, line pie pan and chill. Set oven at hot (425°F).

To make the filling: work cream cheese in a bowl until soft. Beat in the sugar, eggs and cinnamon. Pour into the pastry shell and bake 25 minutes or until the pastry is golden. Cool.

Slice and arrange the peaches on top of the pie.

In a small saucepan melt the preserves, then work through a strainer. Melt again over gentle heat; brush over the peach slices. Serve very cold.

Jam Omelet

6 eggs
2 tablespoons sugar
6 tablespoons apricot, raspberry or strawberry jam
$\frac{1}{4}$ cup butter
$\frac{1}{4}$ cup rum or brandy

Method
Beat eggs and sugar in a bowl with a fork until completely mixed. Melt jam in a small saucepan and set aside. In a large omelet pan melt butter, pour in eggs and cook over high heat, stirring once or twice with the flat of the fork, until omelet is lightly set. Spoon in the jam, fold omelet in half and turn onto a heated platter.

Pour rum or brandy into the saucepan and, heating briefly if necessary, flame it. Pour over the omelet and serve at once.

Toffee French Toast

4–6 hamburger buns, top and bottom crusts removed
1 egg
1 cup milk

For toffee mixture
6 tablespoons butter
6 tablespoons sugar
6 tablespoons light corn syrup
1 cup sour cream or plain yogurt
sugar (to taste)

Method
Beat the egg and milk until mixed. Pour onto a plate and dip the buns in the mixture until absorbed.

To make the toffee mixture: in a skillet or frying pan combine half the butter, half the sugar and half the syrup. Cook, stirring, until mixture starts to brown. At once add the soaked buns, cook until brown on one side, then turn and brown on the other.

Take out the buns and arrange them overlapping in a circle on a buttered dish and keep warm.

Wipe out the pan, cook the remaining toffee ingredients in the same way, and pour or spoon this mixture over the buns. Add sugar to taste to the sour cream or yogurt and spoon into the center of the dish.

Toffee French toast is served with sour cream or plain yogurt

Fondue bourguignonne is accompanied by various dips and savory sauces (recipes on pages 46–49)

Treats for Teenagers

Please all teen-age tastes with one of our three menus. There's the do-it-yourself steak dish, fondue bourguignonne, followed by those all-time favorites, peach and blueberry pies. For a foolproof buffet, you can't go wrong with croquettes of chicken and pineapple, meatballs with tomato and pepper sauce, and cheese, bacon and potato galette. For the teen-age traditionalists who reject such fancy food, serve straightforward hamburgers and ice cream sundaes.

Fondue Bourguignonne
Selection of Fondue Sauces
Garlic Loaf   Green Salad

Peach or Blueberry Pies

Croquettes of Chicken & Pineapple

Meatballs with Tomato & Pepper Sauce

Cheese, Bacon & Potato Galette
Country Cole Slaw

Fresh Fruit

Hamburgers
Selection of Salads,
Mayonnaise & Relishes

Ice Cream Sundaes

MENU 1

Fondue Bourguignonne

Selection of Fondue Sauces

Garlic Loaf

Green Salad

Peach or Blueberry Pies

Quantities given in the recipes on pages 46–53 are enough to serve 8 people.

Fondue Bourguignonne

Beef fillet. $1\frac{1}{2}$–2 lb fillet in the piece. Cut it into 1 inch cubes.
Shrimps. Choose large shrimps in the shell (3–4 per person). Cook them in simmering salted water for 3–4 minutes, drain and peel them before the party.
Chicken. Buy 4–5 chicken pieces – thighs and breast meat are best. Discard the skin and bones, cut chicken in pieces about 1 X 2 inches, season with salt and freshly ground pepper, and add a little lemon juice.

Fondue bourguignonne is ideal for teen-age entertaining because the guests can do the cooking and the hostess needs only to supply the ingredients.

The classic recipe calls for a pan of hot oil that is set over a burner in the center of the table. Guests spear chunks of steak (it must be of top quality or it will be tough) and dip them into the hot oil until cooked to taste. Since the steak is expensive, stretch it by adding shrimps and pieces of chicken.

Savory sauces for flavoring the cooked meat, and crusty rolls, garlic loaf or French bread are the only accompaniments, with a green salad if you like.

The more sauces served, the better your fondue will be. Hollandaise (see recipe for eggs Benedict on page 22), or Béarnaise (see Volume 2) is a must, and Cumberland sauce is also suitable (see Volume 1). Otherwise, take your pick of the special fondue sauces given here.

A flameproof metal pan is normally used as the fat must be heated on the stove before it is transferred to a portable burner; ceramic or earthenware fondue pots are intended for cheese fondue as this requires a lower heat. A short time before serving, half-fill a metal fondue pan with oil or a mixture of equal quantities of oil and butter. Cook over medium heat until the fat is hot enough to brown a small piece of bread in 30 seconds. When oil and butter are used, the fat will sputter as it is warmed and should be heated until this stops. When the fat is hot, transfer the pan to a portable burner and call guests to the table (the burner flame will keep the fat hot but won't heat it initially).

TIMETABLE

Day before
Prepare 4–5 fondue sauces of your choice. Cover with plastic wrap and chill.

Morning
Cut beef or chicken into cubes; cook and peel shrimps. Wash greens for salad and keep in plastic bag in refrigerator.
Remove sauces from refrigerator; check which need reheating. Make and bake pies; make spicy hard sauce if used.
Prepare the garlic loaf and wrap in foil.
Make the vinaigrette dressing for the salad.
Assemble equipment for final cooking from 5:30 for party around 6 p.m.

Order of Work

5:30
Arrange meat, shrimps and chicken on serving dishes.
Transfer cold sauces to their serving dishes.

5:45
Bake garlic loaf.
Reheat all sauces to be served hot.
Start to heat oil in the fondue pot on stove.
Turn oven to lowest possible setting, and warm the pies.
Toss salad at the table.

6:00
Begin the party.

Garlic Loaf

Cut 1 large loaf of French, Italian or regular unsliced white bread into $1\frac{1}{2}$ inch slices, cutting through to within $\frac{1}{2}$ inch of the bottom.

Crush 1–2 cloves of garlic with a pinch of salt in a bowl and work in $\frac{1}{4}$–$\frac{1}{2}$ cup butter (depending on the size of the loaf) until creamy. Spread this garlic butter on either side of each slice of bread, reserving a little butter, and press the loaf back into shape. Spread the top and sides of the loaf with the remaining butter, wrap in foil and bake in a hot oven (400°F) for 12–15 minutes, opening the foil for the last 5 minutes so the bread becomes crisp.

If you prefer just a hint of garlic flavor, cut one clove only into quarters but do not crush it. Cream the butter, add the quartered garlic clove and let stand for 30 minutes. Then remove the garlic and spread the butter on the bread as above.

For an attractive way to serve hot garlic loaf, carefully open the foil and fan the slices

Drinks: serve refreshing floats – tall glasses three-quarters full of cola or root beer, topped with a scoop of vanilla ice cream. For fruit-flavored alternatives, top lemonade with a colorful scoop of orange, lemon or lime sherbet. Serve with a spoon or straw.

Provençal Dip

1 cup ($\frac{1}{4}$ lb) mushrooms, finely chopped
2 tablespoons oil
1 clove of garlic, finely chopped
$\frac{3}{4}$ cup vegetable juice cocktail
$\frac{3}{4}$ cup mayonnaise
salt and pepper

Method

Sauté mushrooms in oil until all the liquid has evaporated and the mushrooms look dry. Stir in the garlic and continue cooking 1 minute. Stir in vegetable juice cocktail and simmer until reduced and mixture thickens. Cool, then stir in the mayonnaise and salt and pepper to taste. Serve cold.

Mustard Cream

2 teaspoons Dijon-style mustard
$\frac{1}{2}$ cup mayonnaise
$\frac{1}{2}$ cup sour cream
salt and pepper
squeeze of lemon juice

Method

In a bowl mix the mustard with mayonniase, stir in the sour cream until smooth and season with salt and pepper. Add lemon juice to taste. Serve cold.

Deviled Tomato Sauce

4 large ripe tomatoes, peeled, seeded and coarsely chopped
$\frac{1}{4}$ cup ketchup
1 tablespoon red wine vinegar
2 tablespoons oil
few drops of Tabasco
salt and pepper
pinch of dry mustard

Method

Combine all ingredients with salt, pepper and mustard to taste. Serve cold.

Mouth-watering peach pie, a simple desert to make, is served with vanilla ice cream

Horseradish Sauce

2 teaspoons freshly grated horseradish, or $1\frac{1}{2}$ tablespoons prepared horseradish
1 tablespoon butter
1 tablespoon flour
$\frac{3}{4}$ cup chicken stock
$\frac{1}{2}$ cup light cream
salt and pepper
dash of cayenne
squeeze of lemon juice

Method

Melt butter in a saucepan, blend in the flour and cook, stirring, until pale straw-colored. Add the chicken stock, stir until the mixture boils and cook for 3 minutes. Add the horseradish and cream and bring back to a boil, stirring constantly. Season with salt and pepper. Add a little cayenne and lemon juice to taste. Serve hot.

Sweet and Sour Sauce

1 green pepper, cored, seeded and coarsely chopped
1 small ($8\frac{1}{4}$ oz) can crushed pineapple
1 tablespoon honey
1 tablespoon red wine vinegar
1 tablespoon soy sauce
$\frac{3}{4}$ cup sour cream
$\frac{3}{4}$ cup boiled dressing (see Volume 4)
salt and pepper
squeeze of lemon juice

Method

Blanch the green pepper in boiling salted water for 1 minute; drain and refresh. When cold, mix it with the pineapple.

Stir honey, vinegar and soy sauce into the sour cream and boiled dressing. Add the pepper and pineapple mixture and season with salt and pepper. Add lemon juice to taste. Serve cold.

Anchovy Mayonnaise

2 teaspoons anchovy paste
1 cup mayonnaise
1 tablespoon chopped parsley, or capers
1 tablespoon chopped dill pickle
1 small clove of garlic, crushed
3 ripe olives, pitted and chopped
1 hard-cooked egg
1–2 tablespoons heavy cream (optional)

Method

Mix the mayonnaise with parsley or capers, anchovy paste and dill pickle. Stir in the garlic and chopped olives. Finely chop egg white and work egg yolk through a sieve; add to anchovy mayonnaise. Taste for seasoning and, if flavor is too tart, stir in a little cream. Serve cold.

Quantities given in the recipes on pages 46–53 are enough to serve 8 people.

Peach and Blueberry Pies

For pie pastry
4 cups flour
$1\frac{1}{3}$ cups shortening
1 teaspoon salt
6–8 tablespoons ice water

For peach filling
1 large can (16 oz) sliced peaches
4 fresh peaches
little butter

For blueberry filling
1 quart fresh or frozen blueberries
1 cup sugar
$\frac{1}{3}$ cup flour
1 teaspoon grated lemon rind
$\frac{1}{8}$ teaspoon salt
2 tablespoons butter

Two 8–9 inch pie pans

Method

Make the pie pastry dough, chill 30 minutes, roll out half in 2 circles and line the pie pans. Set oven at hot (425°F).

Drain canned peaches thoroughly. Scald and peel fresh ones; cut in slices. Combine fresh and canned slices and fill pie shell. Dot the top with butter and moisten edges of pie shell with cold water.

If using blueberries for the second pie, combine them with sugar, flour, lemon rind and salt. Fill second pie shell. Dot the top with butter and moisten the edges of the pie shell with cold water.

Divide remaining dough in half, roll out each half to a circle slightly larger than the pans. Lift circles onto the pies and seal the edges. Cut vents for steam to escape and flute the edges if you like.

Bake pies in heated oven for 15 minutes, then reduce heat to 400°F; continue baking 30–40 minutes or until the pastry is brown and juice bubbles in the steam vents. Serve the pies warm with spicy hard sauce, whipped cream, or vanilla ice cream.

Spicy Hard Sauce

Cream 5 tablespoons butter until soft; sift 1 cup confectioners' sugar and add gradually to butter, beating well until blended. Add large pinch of salt and 1 teaspoon vanilla, $\frac{1}{2}$ teaspoon each of ground cinnamon and lemon juice and $\frac{1}{4}$ teaspoon ground cloves. Beat until blended; chill.

MENU 2

Croquettes of Chicken & Pineapple

Meatballs with Tomato & Pepper Sauce

Cheese, Bacon & Potato Galette

Country Cole Slaw

Fruit Jelly Roll Gelatine

Quantities given in the recipes on these pages are enough to serve 8 people. For suggested drinks, see page 47.

TIMETABLE

Morning
Prepare meatballs and sauce, cook until almost done and refrigerate.
Prepare chicken and pineapple croquettes, arrange in baking dish and refrigerate.
Prepare the galette and cover but do not bake.
Make the dressing for cole slaw and cover.
Check fresh fruit: wipe apples and pears; wash grapes, plums and other relatively soft fruit. Pile in a serving bowl.
Assemble equipment for final cooking from 4:30 for party around 6 p.m.

Order of Work
4:30
Set oven at hot (400°F).
4:45
Uncover the galette and put in oven.
5:15
Turn oven to moderately hot (375°F).
Put chicken and pineapple croquettes in heated oven to bake.
Shred cabbage and toss cole slaw with dressing.
Heat meatballs in sauce on top of the stove.
6:00
Begin the party.

Croquettes of Chicken and Pineapple

2 cups (1 lb) finely chopped cooked chicken, marinated for 30 minutes in 3–4 tablespoons juice from canned pineapple rings and a squeeze of lemon juice
8 canned pineapple rings, drained
1½ cups fresh white breadcrumbs
1 tablespoon chopped chives
salt and pepper
2 eggs, beaten to mix
1 tablespoon butter
2 tablespoons brown sugar
2 tablespoons pineapple juice (from canned pineapple rings)
squeeze of lemon juice
1 tablespoon chopped parsley (for garnish)

Makes 8 large croquettes.

Method
Set oven at moderately hot (375°F).

Mix the marinated chicken, breadcrumbs and chives together. Season with salt and pepper; bind with beaten egg. Shape the mixture into 8 rounds or patties; place each one on a pineapple ring in a buttered baking dish.

Melt the butter in a pan, add brown sugar and blend in pineapple and lemon juices. Spoon the mixture over the croquettes; bake in heated oven for 30–40 minutes or until browned, basting occasionally. Garnish with parsley.

Meatballs with Tomato and Pepper Sauce

1 lb lean beef, ground
⅓ lb pork, ground
1 cup fine dry breadcrumbs
½ cup grated Parmesan cheese
1 tablespoon chopped parsley
2 cloves of garlic, crushed
salt and pepper
2 eggs, beaten to mix
about ½ cup milk
½ cup seasoned flour (made with ½ teaspoon salt and ¼ teaspoon pepper)
3 tablespoons oil

For sauce
1 can (16 oz) tomatoes
2 green peppers, cored, seeded and chopped
2 large onions, chopped
2 tablespoons flour
1 bay leaf
sugar
dash of Worcestershire sauce

Method
To make the meatballs: mix beef and pork with breadcrumbs, cheese, parsley, garlic and seasoning; bind with beaten eggs and enough milk to make a firm mixture. Shape the mixture into balls about 1½ inches in diameter and roll in seasoned flour.

Melt oil in a pan and fry meatballs, a few at a time, until golden brown on all sides; remove and keep warm.

To make the sauce: in the same pan cook onions over low heat until golden. Blend in flour; stir in tomatoes, green peppers, bay leaf, salt, pepper, sugar and Worcestershire sauce to taste. Return the meatballs to pan; cover and simmer 1 hour or until very tender.

Remove bay leaf before serving.

Cheese, Bacon and Potato Galette

¼ lb sliced processed cheese
¼ lb sliced bacon
8 medium potatoes
2 tablespoons butter
salt and pepper
1½–2 cups chicken stock

Method
Set oven at hot (400°F). Cut each slice of cheese into 4 pieces; cut each slice of bacon in half. Peel potatoes and cut them into very thin slices.

Rub half the butter around an ovenproof dish; arrange the potatoes in it, seasoning lightly between the layers. Pour in enough stock almost to cover the potatoes, spread with bacon and cheese on top and dot with remaining butter.

Bake in heated oven for about 1¼ hours or until potatoes are tender and the cheese and bacon are brown and crisp, adding more stock if the dish seems dry.

Country Cole Slaw

1 large firm head of cabbage
1 teaspoon dry mustard
6 tablespoons sugar
$\frac{1}{2}$ teaspoon salt
1 tablespoon flour
$\frac{1}{2}$ cup water
2 eggs
$\frac{1}{2}$ cup cider vinegar
$\frac{1}{4}$ cup butter
1 tablespoon caraway seeds (optional)
little heavy cream (to thin) – optional

Method

Combine mustard, sugar, salt and flour. Stir in $\frac{1}{2}$ cup water to make a smooth mixture. In the top of a double boiler beat the eggs and vinegar together. Stir in the mustard mixture and cook over boiling water until the dressing thickens, stirring frequently. Take pan from the heat. While it is still hot, stir in the butter.

If the dressing is too thick after chilling, thin it with a little heavy cream.

Shred the cabbage finely, discarding the core. Stir in the dressing and caraway seeds, toss well and taste for seasoning.

Fruit Jelly Roll Gelatine

1 can (16 oz) sliced pears or peaches
1 jelly roll, cut in $\frac{1}{2}$ inch slices
1 package of orange gelatine
juice of 1 orange

Glass bowl (2–2$\frac{1}{2}$ quart capacity)

Method

Line the bowl with the sliced jelly roll.

Drain the pears or peaches, reserving the juice, and pile them in the bottom of the bowl. Bring 1 cup of the juice to a boil, pour over the orange gelatine and stir until dissolved. Stir in the orange juice and the remaining fruit juice and let cool.

Pour the gelatine mixture into the lined bowl, cover and chill 2 hours or until set.

For a popular dessert, serve fruit jelly roll gelatine

A hamburger to challenge any teenager, with a radish rose to complete the trimmings

MENU 3

Hamburgers

Selection of Salads, Mayonnaise & Relishes

Ice Cream Sundaes

Quantities given in the recipes on these pages are enough to serve 8 people. For suggested drinks, see page 47.

Hamburgers

3–3½ lb lean chuck or round beef, ground
1 cup fresh white breadcrumbs
½ teaspoon dried thyme
2 teaspoons salt
black pepper, freshly ground
3 eggs, beaten to mix
½ cup butter
8 hamburger buns (to serve)

Method

Split buns and put them into a moderate oven (350°F) for 8–10 minutes or until hot.

Mix the fresh breadcrumbs, thyme and seasoning with the ground beef, add beaten eggs gradually and work the mixture together well. Shape the meat into 8 flat patties the same diameter as the buns. Fry the hamburgers in the butter for 3–4 minutes on each side, or brush them with melted butter and broil until they are well browned.

Put a hot hamburger in the center of a warmed bun and serve at once, leaving each guest to add the accompaniments of his choice.

TIMETABLE

Morning
Prepare hamburgers. Arrange on a baking sheet; cover with plastic wrap; chill.
Prepare all accompaniments for hamburgers and, where necessary, chill.
Check ingredients for sundaes: chop nuts, crush peppermint candy, whip cream, wash and hull strawberries.
Assemble equipment for final cooking from 5:15 for party around 6 p.m.

Order of Work

5:15
Remove hamburgers from refrigerator.
Arrange the hamburger accompaniments on table.
Set the ice cream accompaniments on table.
Slit hamburger buns; arrange on a baking sheet to be heated.

5:45
Put buns in oven to warm.
Start cooking hamburgers, not too many at a time.
As each is cooked, place in heated bun.

6:00
Begin the party.

Accompaniments to Hamburgers

A bowl of crisp lettuce leaves; slices of tomato; very thin slices of raw Bermuda onions; radish roses.

Bowls of mayonnaise; ketchup; prepared mustard; dill pickles (sliced); coarsely chopped beets mixed with a little prepared horseradish, mayonnaise and lemon juice; corn or green pepper relish.

Radish Roses

Trim the tails and all but the smallest green leaves from red radishes. With a sharp knife, make several angled cuts (like tiny petals) down the radish, starting at the root end and working down to the stem end, but do not slice completely through.

When prepared, keep the radishes in a bowl of ice water so the petals open out.

Ice Cream Sundaes

Coffee Sundae

Top scoops of coffee ice cream with maple syrup and coarsely chopped walnuts.

Hot Fudge Sundae

Pour hot fudge sauce over the vanilla ice cream and sprinkle with crushed peppermint candy.

Orange Strawberry Sundae

Surround orange sherbet with fresh strawberries and top with whipped cream.

Banana Split

Split banana in half, then arrange scoops of vanilla and strawberry ice cream on top of each half. Top with a little hot fudge sauce, whipped cream and chopped nuts.

Fudge Sauce

1 package (12 oz) semisweet chocolate pieces
2 squares (2 oz) unsweetened chocolate
3 tablespoons strong coffee
1 cup heavy cream

Method

Put both kinds of chocolate and the coffee in the top of a double boiler. Let the chocolate melt over the hot water, then gradually stir in the cream until smooth. Serve hot or cool.

Braised round of beef on a mirepoix of vegetables (recipe is on page 60)

HOW TO BRAISE

Braising is an ideal way to cook less expensive cuts of meat that are full of flavor but inclined to be tough. When braising, it is essential to use a very small quantity of liquid in a pot with a tight fitting lid so that the meat cooks in the steam from the liquid. This keeps the meat moist and at the end of cooking, it is tender and succulent with a rich strong gravy.

Sometimes, before cooking, meat is larded: strips of salt pork are inserted into the meat to add flavor and richness. Or the meat may be barded, when a sheet of pork fat is tied around it. Most of the cooking is done in the oven so that the meat is heated from both top and bottom. The pot you choose is important: it should be made of enameled iron, cast iron or thick aluminum and must be deep enough so meat fits snugly into it. Ovenware that is not flameproof cannot be used because part of the cooking is done on top of the stove.

Cuts for Braising

Beef	Heel of round, round, sirloin tip, rump, flank, chuck (blade), shoulder, arm, brisket
Lamb	Leg (plain or boned and stuffed), loin or breast (boned and stuffed), foreshank
Pork	(Cured) ham, Canadian bacon, smoked hock; (fresh) pork steak, hind foot, sirloin roast, tenderloin, blade loin, Boston butt, picnic shoulder, hock, forefoot
Veal	Heel of round, flank, blade steak, arm (cuts may be plain or stuffed)
Poultry	Chicken, duck, goose, turkey
Game	Saddle or haunch of venison, squab, pheasant, wild duck, quail, rabbit

Braising Fish

Braising is an excellent way to cook whole fish such as haddock or scrod (baby cod) or large pieces of fish. If you like, first stuff the fish with a herb mixture, then lay it on the mirepoix of vegetables. Pour over $\frac{1}{2}$ cup of cider, white wine or water; add a little salt and pepper and a bouquet garni. Cover the pot tightly and braise in a moderately low oven (325°F).

Allow 15–20 minutes per lb for large fish and about 20–25 minutes total cooking time for small fish like red snapper or trout. When the fish is cooked, drain and keep hot. Strain the cooking liquid and thicken it with a little arrowroot mixed to a paste with water. Spoon this sauce over the fish and sprinkle generously with chopped parsley.

The traditional **braisière** (or pan for braising) was designed for stoves without an oven. It has an indented lid in which live coals were placed so that the pan was heated from the top as well as the bottom. Braising pans are still sometimes made in this shape, although the indented lid is no longer necessary.

For jellied stock, long, slow simmering is essential. Stock should never be boiled hard or it will be thick and muddy instead of clear.

Braising Meat, Poultry and Game

In a deep flameproof casserole, heat 2 tablespoons oil over moderate heat and brown the meat, poultry or game on all sides. Take it out, add about 2 cups vegetables, diced or sliced (this is called a mirepoix). The vegetables may include onion, carrot, celery and a little turnip or leek.

Cover the pot and cook gently (or sweat) for 5–7 minutes. This allows the juice to run from the vegetables and lets them absorb the fat. Replace the meat, poultry or game on top of the mirepoix with a bouquet garni and a little salt and pepper.

Pour in the liquid called for in the particular recipe – this should fill the bottom of the pot up to a level of 2–3 inches. Cover the pot tightly and bake in a moderately low oven (325°F), allowing 25–35 minutes per lb, depending on the thickness of the cut, and 30 minutes extra time. Cuts like leg of lamb, that are tender enough to be roasted, will take less time than tough braising cuts. For tender cuts allow 20 minutes per lb plus an extra 20 minutes.

When braising birds, allow 20 minutes per lb, plus an extra 20 minutes. Goose or duck may take longer if very fatty.

Baste and turn the meat occasionally – it should be very tender when cooked.

When the meat is done, remove it from the pot and keep warm. Strain the gravy and skim it thoroughly to remove any fat, taking particular care when cooking duck or goose. Depending on the recipe, a sauce may be added or the gravy may be thickened with kneaded butter or arrowroot.

Normally the vegetables cooked with the meat or poultry are discarded because they become overcooked and their flavor has been passed on to the gravy. However, when a roasting cut of meat or game is braised, the cooking time is shorter and the vegetables that were cooked with the meat can be served with it.

Watchpoint: when braising, it is important to use jellied brown stock. If the stock is not strong, add a pig's foot to the pot, tucking it down beside the meat. This gives a delicious flavor and glossy appearance to the finished sauce.

Braising Vegetables

Onion, celery, endive, leeks, cabbage and lettuce are all good vegetables for braising. Blanch them (for root vegetables, put in cold water and bring to a boil; for green vegetables, put in boiling water and bring to a boil again before draining thoroughly). This blanching removes any strong flavor and softens the outside of the vegetables so they cook thoroughly.

Note: a recipe for braised leeks was given in Volume 1.

Thickening Agents

Arrowroot, cornstarch and potato starch are similar thickening agents, and are most often used when the exact amount of liquid to be thickened is unknown; for example, after braising meat the quantity of gravy remaining depends on the amount of evaporation during cooking.

Arrowroot, cornstarch and potato starch should all be mixed with a little cold liquid to a smooth paste (known as a liaison), then gradually whisked into the hot liquid to be thickened. Add only enough paste to give liquid the right consistency.

Arrowroot is best used for clear sauces or fruit syrups because it will be clear once it has thickened.

Potato starch acts like arrowroot but is not as clear. Both will thicken a liquid as soon as it comes to a boil, but if boiled for a minute or more, the liquid tends to thin the longer it cooks.

Cornstarch is best used for custards and thick white coating sauces. It becomes thicker the longer it cooks.

Braised Salmon

2–3 lb center cut piece of salmon
2 tablespoons butter
2 medium onions, diced
1 cup sherry
1 cup fish stock or water
bouquet garni
6 peppercorns
kneaded butter (made with $1\frac{1}{2}$ tablespoons butter and $\frac{3}{4}$ tablespoon flour)

For stuffing
2 tablespoons butter
2 medium carrots, finely diced
1 large onion, finely diced
2 teaspoons flour
2–3 tablespoons heavy cream
2 truffles with their liquid, diced (optional)
salt and pepper

Method

To make the stuffing: melt the butter, add carrots and onion and cook over very low heat until the vegetables are soft but not browned. Stir in the flour and cook 1 minute. Stir in enough cream to make a soft mixture and cook gently for 1 minute. Take from the heat, stir in the truffles (with their liquid), if used, and season to taste. Cool.

Wipe the salmon with a damp cloth and fill the cavity with the stuffing.

In a deep flameproof casserole, melt the butter and cook onions, covered, over low heat for 5–7 minutes until very soft and transparent. Place the salmon on top, pour over the sherry and fish stock or water, add bouquet garni and peppercorns and cover the pot. Braise in a moderately low oven (325°F) for 35–45 minutes or until the salmon is no longer transparent in the center when flaked with a fork. Drain, remove the skin and keep warm on a platter.

Strain the cooking liquid and bring it to a boil. Whisk in the kneaded butter, a little at a time, until the sauce is the consistency of light cream. Taste for seasoning, spoon a little over the salmon and serve the rest separately.

Braised Fish à la Bourguignonne

4 lb whole cod, or striped bass
1 tablespoon oil
$\frac{1}{4}$ lb piece of bacon, diced and blanched
2 medium onions, chopped
1 cup red wine
1 cup water
bouquet garni
2 cups ($\frac{1}{2}$ lb) quartered mushrooms
kneaded butter (made with 1 tablespoon butter and $\frac{1}{2}$ tablespoon flour)
salt and pepper

If using a more delicate fish like flounder for this recipe, add white wine instead of red.

Method

In an oval flameproof casserole, heat the oil and lightly brown the bacon and onions. Drain off excess fat, put in the fish and add wine, water and bouquet garni. Cover and braise in a moderately low oven (325°F) for 20 minutes. Add the mushrooms and continue cooking for 15–20 minutes or until the fish flakes easily when tested with a fork.

Remove the bouquet garni, and transfer the fish to a platter.

Thicken the sauce lightly by stirring in the kneaded butter, bring to a boil, taste for seasoning and spoon the sauce and vegetables over the fish.

Braised Turkey Alsacienne

6–8 lb turkey
thin slice of pork fat (for barding)
3 tablespoons butter
2 medium onions, diced
2 carrots, diced
4 stalks of celery, diced
1 cup white wine
1 cup well-flavored chicken stock
bouquet garni
salt and pepper
1 teaspoon arrowroot (mixed to a paste with 1 tablespoon water) – optional
1 lb knockwurst (for garnish)

Method

Lay the pork fat over the breast of the turkey and tie it with string.

In a deep flameproof casserole, heat the butter and cook the onions, carrots and celery, covered, over low heat for 5–7 minutes. Place the turkey on top pour over the wine and stock and add bouquet garni and seasoning. Cover the pot and braise in a moderately low oven (325°F) for 2–3 hours or until the turkey is very tender.

Transfer the bird to a platter, discard the pork fat and keep warm. Strain the cooking liquid and reduce it by boiling until it is glossy and concentrated in flavor. Season to taste and thicken, if you like, by stirring in the arrowroot paste.

Immerse the knockwurst in a pan of hot water and poach just below simmering point for 10 minutes or until thoroughly heated. Drain.

Spoon a little of the gravy over the turkey and serve the rest separately. Arrange the knockwurst around the turkey and serve with braised sauerkraut (see recipe on page 64).

Braised chicken with morel mushrooms and small potatoes is cooked in a red wine sauce

Poulet Braisé aux Morilles
(Braised Chicken with Morels)

Morels are dark wrinkled mushrooms with a rich aromatic flavor. They grow wild in many areas of the U.S.A. but are very hard to find, so they are expensive. They are available dried or in cans.

4–5 lb roasting chicken or fowl
$\frac{3}{4}$ cup dried or 1 can (12 oz) morel mushrooms
6–8 small potatoes

For braising
1 tablespoon oil
1 tablespoon butter
1 onion, diced
1 carrot, diced
1 cup red wine
1 cup stock
bouquet garni
salt and pepper

Method

Soak the dried morels in warm water to cover for 30 minutes and drain, or drain canned morels.

In a flameproof casserole heat the oil and butter and brown the bird on all sides. Take out, add the onion and carrot, cover the pot and cook gently for 5–7 minutes. Replace the bird, add the wine, stock, bouquet garni, seasoning and morels. Cover and braise in a moderate oven (350°F) for 1–1$\frac{1}{4}$ hours for the chicken or 1$\frac{1}{2}$–1$\frac{3}{4}$ hours for the fowl or until almost tender. Add the potatoes and cook 20–30 minutes longer or until the potatoes and chicken are tender.

Ris de Veau Braisé au Vin Blanc
(Braised Sweetbreads with White Wine)

2–3 pairs (about 1$\frac{1}{2}$ lb) calves' sweetbreads
$\frac{1}{2}$ cup white wine
slice of lemon
kneaded butter, made with 1 tablespoon butter and $\frac{1}{2}$ tablespoon flour

For braising
1 tablespoon butter
2 onions, thinly sliced
2 carrots, thinly sliced
2 stalks of celery, thinly sliced
$\frac{1}{2}$ cup stock
1 teaspoon tomato paste
bouquet garni
salt and pepper

For garnish
morels or mushrooms with cream (see right)

Variety meats and veal are sometimes braised 'à blanc' – that is, the vegetables and meat are not browned before cooking.

Method

Soak the sweetbreads for 2–3 hours in cold water with a slice of lemon. Drain them, rinse and put them in a pan. Cover with cold water, add a little salt and bring to a boil over low heat, skimming them occasionally.

Drain and rinse the sweetbreads and remove any ducts and skin that will pull off easily. Press the sweetbreads between 2 plates with a 2 lb weight on top and leave until they are cold.

Spread a sauté pan or shallow casserole with the butter. Add the vegetables and set the sweetbreads on top. Pour over the wine and stock and add the tomato paste, bouquet garni and seasoning. Cover and braise in a moderate oven (350°F) for $\frac{3}{4}$–1 hour or until the sweetbreads are very tender.

Lift out the sweetbreads, carve them in $\frac{1}{2}$ inch slices and arrange them, overlapping, down one side of a platter; keep warm.

Strain the cooking liquid into a saucepan and skim off any fat. Bring to a boil and add the kneaded butter, a small piece at a time, whisking until the sauce thickens slightly. Taste for seasoning and spoon over the sweetbreads.

Spoon morels or mushrooms with cream down the other side of the platter, and serve with potato croquettes.

Potato Croquettes

Cook 5 medium potatoes in boiling salted water for 15 minutes or until tender. Drain. Work through a strainer or ricer. Return to pan, beat in 2 tablespoons butter, 2 egg yolks, $\frac{1}{4}$ cup hot milk, salt and pepper.

Cool the potato mixture, roll out onto a floured board into a 1 inch thick cylinder. Cut into 2 inch lengths. Roll the croquettes in flour, seasoned with salt and pepper, and brush them with 1 egg, beaten to mix with $\frac{1}{2}$ teaspoon salt.

Coat the potato croquettes with dry white breadcrumbs. Fry them in butter, turning so they brown evenly, or fry them in hot deep fat (375°F on a fat thermometer) until golden brown. Drain well on paper towels. Serves 6.

Morilles à la Crème
(Morels with Cream)

1$\frac{1}{2}$ cups dried or 2 cans (12 oz each) morel mushrooms
1$\frac{1}{2}$ cups heavy cream
2 tablespoons butter
1 tablespoon flour
salt and pepper
$\frac{1}{4}$ teaspoon nutmeg
$\frac{1}{2}$ cup sour cream

Button mushrooms may be substituted for morels in this recipe. Use 1 lb small mushrooms and trim the stems. Sauté them in butter and continue cooking as for morels.

Serves 6 as an appetizer on toast or in a pastry shell. Serves 6–8 as an accompaniment to an entrée.

Method

Soak dried morels in warm water to cover for 30 minutes and drain, or drain canned morels. Dry them on paper towels.

Heat the butter, add the morels and sauté 2 minutes. Stir in the flour, add the heavy cream and bring to a boil, stirring. Season with salt, pepper and nutmeg and simmer 2 minutes or until the sauce is fairly thick.

Just before serving, stir in the sour cream and reheat without boiling.

Braised Round of Beef

3–3½ lb round of beef

For braising
1–2 tablespoons oil or beef drippings
2 onions, sliced or diced
2 carrots, sliced or diced
2 stalks of celery, sliced or diced
bouquet garni
salt and pepper
¾ cup jellied stock

For sauce
1½ tablespoons oil or beef drippings
1 tablespoon flour
2 cups stock
1 teaspoon tomato paste

Brisket may be substituted for round but has more fat. If you prefer leaner meat, use sirloin tip, rump, or a well trimmed chuck roast.

Method
In a deep flameproof casserole, heat 1–2 tablespoons oil or drippings. When hot, put in the meat; brown on all sides. Take out, lower heat and add vegetables. Cover and cook gently for 5–7 minutes.

Place the meat on top of the vegetables, add bouquet garni and seasoning and pour in stock. Cover and braise in a moderately low oven (325°F) for 1½–2 hours or until meat is tender.

To make the sauce: in a saucepan heat the oil or drippings, stir in the flour and cook slowly, stirring, until the flour is deep brown, but do not let it scorch. Let cool slightly, then stir in stock and add tomato paste. Bring to a boil and simmer sauce, uncovered, for 15–20 minutes.

When the meat is tender, take it from the pot, slice what is needed, arrange it on a platter and keep hot. Any remaining meat should be pressed between 2 heavy plates (this makes the meat easier to carve) and eaten cold.

Strain the gravy from the pot and skim well to remove the fat. Add the gravy to the sauce and reduce it by boiling until glossy and the consistency of heavy cream. Season and spoon enough over meat to moisten it. Serve the rest separately. Accompany braised round of beef with boiled or baked potatoes and a root vegetable like carrots, parsnips or turnips.

Paupiettes de Boeuf Braisées à la Crème
(Beef Roulades in Sour Cream)

6 large thin slices (about 2 lb) round or chuck steak
½ cup sour cream
1 tablespoon chopped parsley (for garnish)

For stuffing
2 tablespoons freshly grated horseradish or ¼ cup prepared horseradish
½ cup fresh white breadcrumbs
1 egg
salt and pepper

For braising
1 tablespoon oil
1 tablespoon butter
1 onion, diced
1 carrot, diced
1 tablespoon flour
1½ cups beef stock
bouquet garni

Method
Pound the slices of beef between 2 sheets of wax paper, using a rolling pin or heavy pan. Trim and cut each slice in half.

Combine all the ingredients for the stuffing, season and spread on the slices of beef. Roll them up neatly and tie with string.

In a flameproof casserole heat the oil and butter and brown the beef roulades on all sides. Take them out, add the onion and carrot, cover the pot and cook gently for 5–7 minutes. Sprinkle with flour, replace the roulades, add the stock, bouquet garni and seasoning, cover and braise in a low oven (325°F) for 1¼–1½ hours or until the roulades are tender. Transfer the roulades to a platter, remove the strings and keep warm.

Strain the cooking liquid into a pan and boil until it is reduced to 1 cup. Stir in the sour cream and reheat without boiling. Taste for seasoning, spoon the sauce over the beef roulades and sprinkle with chopped parsley. Serve with mashed potatoes.

Braised Beef Provençale

3–3½ lb round or sirloin tip of beef
3 tablespoons olive oil or cooking oil
1 large onion, sliced or diced
1 large carrot, sliced or diced
1 clove of garlic, peeled
6 peppercorns
bouquet garni
½ cup red wine
¾ cup jellied stock
salt and pepper

For sauce
1 tablespoon oil
1 tablespoon flour
¾ cup jellied stock

For garnish
4 medium tomatoes, peeled, seeded and cut in quarters
6–8 large green olives, pitted

Method
In a deep flameproof casserole, brown the beef in the oil, then remove it. Add the onion and carrot, lower the heat, cover, and cook slowly for 5–7 minutes until the vegetables are lightly browned but still moist. Place the meat on top of the vegetables, add garlic clove (whole), peppercorns, bouquet garni, wine and stock. Season very lightly, cover tightly and braise in a moderately low oven (325°F) for 1½–2 hours or until the meat is very tender.

To make the sauce: heat the oil, stir in the flour and cook over medium heat until flour is deep brown. Take from the heat, stir in the stock, bring to a boil and simmer 7–10 minutes.

Take the meat from the pot, strain the gravy and skim it to remove the fat. Add the gravy to the sauce and boil to reduce until it is well flavored and the consistency of heavy cream. Take from the heat and adjust seasoning.

Slice the meat, arrange on a deep platter and keep hot. Add tomatoes to the sauce with the olives, whole or quartered, reheat it and spoon over the meat. Serve with mashed potatoes and braised onions (see page 64).

Carve braised beef provençale in slices, add tomatoes and green olives to the rich brown sauce and serve with mashed potatoes

Braised leg of lamb bretonne is a delicious way of cooking a large cut of meat

Braised Leg of Lamb Bretonne

small (4–5 lb) leg of lamb
1 tablespoon oil or meat drippings
1 onion, sliced
2 stalks of celery, sliced
3 large tomatoes, peeled, seeded and chopped, or 1 box cherry tomatoes, peeled
1 clove of garlic, crushed
salt and pepper
$\frac{1}{2}$–$\frac{3}{4}$ cup red or white wine, or stock
bouquet garni

Method
In a deep flameproof casserole heat the oil or drippings and brown lamb on all sides. Place onion, celery, tomatoes and garlic around the meat, season and pour over $\frac{1}{2}$ cup of the wine or stock. Add bouquet garni, cover pot and braise in a moderately low oven (325°F) for 2–2$\frac{1}{2}$ hours or until the lamb is very tender. If the liquid evaporates during cooking, add more wine or stock.

Carve meat and arrange on a platter; remove bouquet garni, taste vegetable mixture for seasoning, add more wine or stock if it is very thick and spoon around meat. Serve with pea beans in cream sauce.

Cream Sauce
For 1$\frac{1}{2}$ cup quantity: melt 3 tablespoons butter, stir in 3 tablespoons flour off the heat and pour in 1$\frac{1}{2}$ cups milk. Bring to a boil, stirring constantly, then let simmer for 2 minutes. Take from heat, season with salt and pepper and add 2–3 tablespoons light cream.

Pea Beans in Cream Sauce

1 cup dried pea beans
small bunch of celery, sliced
12 baby onions, peeled
1 tablespoon chopped parsley
1$\frac{1}{2}$ cups cream sauce (for serving)

Method
Wash the pea beans thoroughly, cover with cold water and soak overnight or prepare according to the package directions.

Put the pea beans in a pan with the celery and onions. Cover with cold water, bring to a boil, cover pan and simmer very gently for 1$\frac{1}{2}$–2 hours or until the beans are tender.

Drain the bean mixture and add to the cream sauce with chopped parsley. Transfer to a casserole for serving.

Fricandeau with Spinach Purée

3–3$\frac{1}{2}$ lb leg or shoulder of veal, boned
$\frac{1}{4}$ lb piece of salt pork
4–5 slices of bacon
2 large carrots, cut into rounds
2 large onions, cut into rounds
$\frac{1}{2}$ cup white wine
1$\frac{1}{2}$–2 cups jellied stock
salt and pepper
bouquet garni

For spinach purée
1$\frac{1}{2}$ lb fresh spinach
1–2 tablespoons heavy cream, or cream sauce (see box)

Method
Cut salt pork into strips about $\frac{1}{4}$ inch wide and 1$\frac{1}{2}$ inches long. Thread them into a larding needle and lard the piece of veal. Tie the veal with string to form a neat cylinder.

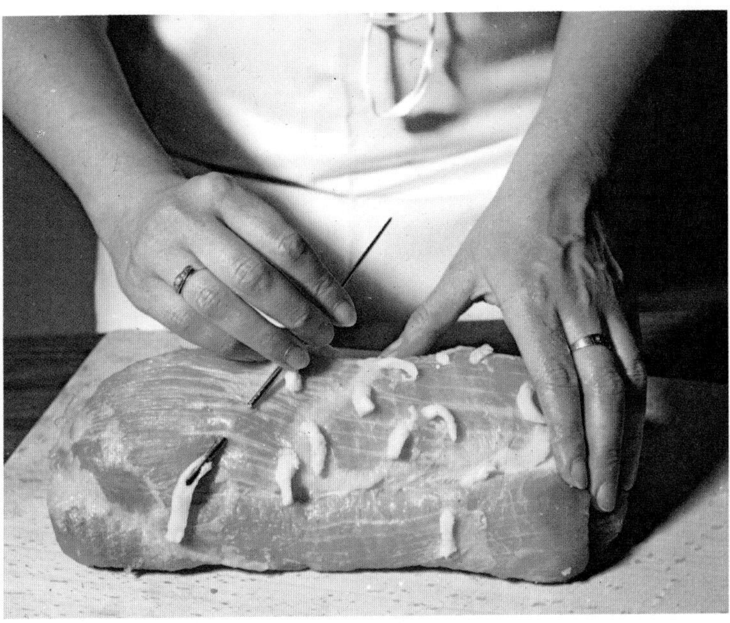

Sew a leg or shoulder of veal for a fricandeau with lardons of pork fat to prevent meat, that has only a little natural fat, from drying out

Lay the bacon in a deep flameproof casserole, put vegetables on top, cover and cook gently for 5–7 minutes. Put in the veal, add the wine, stock, seasoning and bouquet garni and bring to a boil. Cover the pot and braise in a moderately low oven (325°F) for 1–1$\frac{1}{2}$ hours, basting frequently. If the stock reduces fast, add more.

When the meat is tender, remove it, strain the gravy and skim off the fat. Return meat and gravy to the pot and boil on top of the stove for a few minutes, basting to glaze the meat a little. Remove meat and keep hot. If necessary, boil the gravy until it is well reduced and glossy. Taste for seasoning.

To make the spinach purée: wash the spinach thoroughly and cook in boiling salted water for 5 minutes or until just tender. Drain spinach and press well with a spoon or plate to remove as much water as possible. Work it through a sieve and add the cream or cream sauce; alternatively, purée it in a blender with the cream or cream sauce.

Spoon spinach purée down the center of a platter, carve the meat and arrange it on top. Spoon over the gravy.

Fricandeau
This classic French dish is a perfect example of braising. When trimmed and tied, the cut of veal should be 9–11 inches long and 2–3 inches thick.

The traditional accompaniment is a purée of sorrel and spinach, or leaf or puréed spinach. Sorrel is a herb with an acid taste which is delicious combined with spinach or other greens.

Braised Lamb with Pineapple

3–4 lb boned shoulder of lamb
1 small fresh pineapple
bunch of watercress (for garnish)

For braising
1 tablespoon oil
1 tablespoon butter
1 onion, sliced
1 carrot, sliced
2 cups Sauternes or other sweet white wine
bouquet garni
salt and pepper

Fresh pineapple is essential for this recipe as canned pineapple is too sweet.

Method

Peel and cut the pineapple, discarding the skin and core (see box). Slice the pineapple flesh thinly.

With a sharp knife, cut between the skin and the meat of the lamb and insert the slices of pineapple. Roll the shoulder and tie it firmly with string.

In a flameproof casserole brown the lamb in the oil and butter. Remove it, add the onion and carrot, cover and cook gently for 5–7 minutes. Replace the lamb, add the wine, bouquet garni and seasoning. Cover and braise in a moderately low oven (325°F) for $1\frac{1}{2}$–2 hours or until the lamb is tender. Transfer it to a platter and keep warm.

Strain the cooking liquid, pressing the vegetables well to extract all the juice, and skim off any fat. Bring to a boil, taste for seasoning, spoon a little sauce over the lamb and serve the rest separately. Garnish the platter with watercress, and serve with pilaf (see Volume 2).

To Peel and Cut Fresh Pineapple

Slice off the bottom of the pineapple with a serrated-edge knife. Hold pineapple firmly and with a sharp stainless steel knife cut down between the 'eyes' at a 45° angle. The pineapple eyes should come out easily in strips. Remove the plume, slice the flesh thinly and cut out the core with an apple corer. This method disposes of the 'eyes' but avoids waste.

Braised Lettuce

2–4 heads of romaine lettuce (depending on size)
2 tablespoons butter
2 slices of bacon
6 scallions, finely chopped
1–$1\frac{1}{2}$ cups stock
bouquet garni
salt and pepper
1 tablespoon chopped parsley

Method

Wash the lettuces, keeping them whole; trim each base without detaching the outer leaves. If the lettuces are very large, cut in half lengthwise.

Blanch the lettuces in boiling salted water, drain, refresh with cold water and drain again. Generously butter a deep casserole, lay slices of bacon in the bottom and sprinkle over the scallions. Fold the tops of the lettuces under to make a neat shape and lay them on the bacon. Pour over the stock, add bouquet garni and seasoning, and cover the lettuces with buttered foil pressed down on them, then the lid. Braise in a moderate oven (350°F) for 40–45 minutes.

Drain the lettuces and arrange on a platter; keep hot.

Boil the cooking liquid until well reduced and glossy. Strain over the lettuces, sprinkle with parsley and serve.

Braised Sauerkraut

4 cups fresh or canned sauerkraut
6 slices of bacon
1 onion, diced
1 carrot, diced
8 juniper berries, tied in a piece of cheesecloth
bouquet garni
1–$1\frac{1}{4}$ cups stock

Sauerkraut literally means sour or fermented cabbage – the cabbage is finely sliced and fermented in brine for 4–6 weeks. Sauerkraut is sold uncooked, or cooked ready to heat. It can be braised, as we do here, or baked, to accompany spareribs, ham, frankfurters or roast pork and turkey.

Method

Wash sauerkraut thoroughly and drain it well.

In a deep casserole lay 3 slices of the bacon and spread the onion and carrot on top. Put in the sauerkraut and bury the juniper berries in it. Lay the remaining bacon on top with the bouquet garni. Pour over the stock and cover the pot. Braise in a moderately low oven (325°F) for 2 hours or until the sauerkraut is tender and mellow in flavor.

Add more stock during cooking if the sauerkraut looks dry. Remove the juniper berries and bouquet garni before serving.

Braised Onions in Wine

8 medium or 16 baby onions, peeled
1 tablespoon oil
1 carrot, diced
2 stalks of celery, diced
$\frac{1}{2}$ cup red or white wine
$\frac{1}{2}$ cup water
bouquet garni
salt and pepper

Method

Blanch the onions and drain them.

In a deep flameproof casserole, heat the oil and cook carrot and celery, covered, over low heat for 5–7 minutes. Place onions on top, pour over the wine and water, add bouquet garni and seasoning and bring to a boil. Cover pot and braise in a moderately low oven (325°F) for 30–60 minutes (depending on size of onions) or until they are tender. Drain the onions and place in a serving dish or casserole, if you like.

Reduce the cooking liquid, if necessary, by boiling until it is glossy and slightly thick. Taste for seasoning and strain it over the onions.

Braised onions in wine are an ideal accompaniment to braised beef provençale

Marinate chuck roast of beef in red wine, oil, vegetables, garlic and peppercorns before braising (recipe is on page 68)

HOW TO MARINATE

Marinating is the process of soaking meat, game or fish in a mixture of wine, oil, vegetables, herbs and spices. A marinade not only adds flavor but also softens the fibers when meat or game is tough.

Marinades containing wine and vegetables (for large cuts of meat) are usually brought to a boil and left to cool completely before being poured over the meat. For smaller pieces like steaks and fish fillets, a quick, uncooked marinade can be used.

To make the most of a marinade, the meat should fit snugly into a bowl or deep dish. Do not use aluminum containers for marinating because the mixture may develop a metallic taste. Keep the mixture in the refrigerator and turn the meat occasionally. Make sure the vegetables lie on top of the meat to keep it moist. Beef or lamb should be left in a boiled marinade for 24 hours and game can be marinated for up to 3 days. Soaking time for uncooked marinades is much shorter – 2–3 hours is sufficient for steak or fish.

At the end of soaking, the marinade may be used for cooking the meat, or you can brush it over the meat during broiling or add it to a sauce for serving.

Marinade for Beef

For a 3–4 lb cut
2 cloves of garlic, peeled
2 medium onions, thinly sliced
2 medium carrots, thinly sliced
2 stalks of celery, thinly sliced (optional)
10–12 peppercorns
bouquet garni
3 tablespoons olive oil
1½ cups red wine (a Burgundy or any robust red wine)

Method
Bruise the garlic cloves or crush them if you prefer a stronger flavor. Combine with the remaining ingredients, cover and bring to a boil. Simmer 2 minutes, pour into a bowl and cool.

Braised Beef with Red Wine

3–3½ lb rump, lean chuck or sirloin tip of beef
marinade for beef

For braising
½ cup red Burgundy wine
2 tablespoons oil or beef drippings
1 large onion, sliced
1 large carrot, sliced
bouquet garni
clove of garlic, peeled
salt and pepper
¾ cup jellied stock

For sauce
1½ tablespoons oil
1½ tablespoons flour
1½ cups stock
1 teaspoon tomato paste
2 cups (½ lb) small mushrooms

For garnish
12–16 small onions
1 tablespoon butter
1 teaspoon sugar

Method
Prepare the marinade, cool and soak meat in it, covered, in the refrigerator for 24 hours. Take meat from the marinade and pat it dry with paper towels.

In a deep flameproof casserole, heat the oil or drippings and brown the meat on all sides. Take it out, add the onion and carrot, lower the heat and cook gently for 5–7 minutes until browned. Replace the meat, add bouquet garni, garlic (whole or crushed, depending on the strength of flavor you like) and seasoning. Pour in the wine and stock, cover pot and braise in a moderately low oven (325°F) for 2–2½ hours or until the meat is very tender.

To make the sauce: heat the oil, stir in the flour and cook over medium heat until very brown. Take pan from heat, add the stock and tomato paste and strain in the marinade. Bring the sauce to a boil and simmer 15–20 minutes, skimming occasionally to remove any fat.

Wipe the mushrooms with a damp cloth and trim the stalks level with the caps. Add to the sauce and simmer 3–4 minutes.

To prepare the garnish: peel the small onions, cook them in boiling water for 1–2 minutes, then plunge in cold water and drain.

Watchpoint: trim off as little root and top as possible or onions will fall to pieces during cooking – a crosscut in the root end after peeling also helps to prevent this. Put onions in a pan with the butter and sugar and cook gently shaking the pan occasionally, for 6–7 minutes or until the onions are tender and glazed with brown caramel.

When cooked, take the beef from the pot, slice it and keep hot. Boil the cooking liquid to reduce it a little, strain into the sauce and taste for seasoning. Spoon a little over the meat to moisten it and serve the rest separately. Garnish the dish with the glazed onions.

Sauerbraten

3–4 lb piece of round, rump or lean chuck beef
2 tablespoons oil or beef drippings
1 carrot, diced
1 onion, diced
3 stalks of celery, diced
2 tablespoons flour
¾ cup sour cream (optional)
salt and pepper

For marinade
1 tablespoon dry mustard
¾ cup red wine vinegar
¾ cup red wine
1½ cups water
1 medium carrot, sliced
1 medium onion, sliced
2 tablespoons dark brown sugar
2 cloves
1 bay leaf
6 peppercorns
1 teaspoon dried thyme

If you prefer, ¼ cup more vinegar and ½ cup more water may be substituted for the wine.

Method
To prepare the marinade: mix the mustard with a little of the vinegar, then put it in an enamel or stainless steel pan, with remaining ingredients. Bring to a boil, stirring, then let it cool. Put the beef in a deep glass or enamel bowl and pour over the cold marinade. Cover and leave in the refrigerator for 2–3 days, turning the meat occasionally. When ready to cook, take out the beef and pat it dry with paper towels. Strain the marinade and reserve it and the vegetables, but discard the cloves, bay leaf and peppercorns.

In a deep flameproof casserole, heat oil or drippings and brown meat on all sides. Remove it, add carrot, onion and celery and strained vegetables from the marinade, cover and cook 5–7 minutes. Replace the meat, pour over the marinade, cover and bring to a boil. Braise in a moderately low oven (325°F) for 2–2½ hours or until meat is very tender.

Take out the meat and keep warm. Strain the gravy and skim off any fat. Stir a little gravy into the flour to make a smooth mixture and add to the remaining gravy. Bring the sauce back to a boil, stirring, and simmer 2 minutes. Add the sour cream if used, off the heat, reheat the sauce without boiling and season to taste. Carve the meat, spoon a little sauce over and serve the rest separately. Serve with potato dumplings.

Potato Dumplings

4 medium potatoes
1 slice of bread, crusts removed
1–2 tablespoons butter
large pinch of ground mace
1 small egg, beaten to mix
$\frac{1}{2}$ cup flour
1 tablespoon cornstarch
salt and pepper
3–4 tablespoons melted butter (for serving)

Makes 18–20 dumplings.

Method

Wash the potatoes and cook them, unpeeled, in boiling water for 15–20 minutes or until tender. Drain, peel and work through a sieve or mash them until smooth. Leave to cool.

Cut the bread in cubes, fry in the butter until golden brown and drain on paper towels. Add mace, egg, flour, cornstarch and seasoning to the potato. Mix well and shape into balls $1\frac{1}{2}$ inches in diameter. Press 2 cubes of fried bread into the middle of each dumpling, making sure the potato covers the bread completely.

Put the dumplings in a large pan of boiling salted water, taking care not to fill the pan too full – there should be only one layer of potato balls. Simmer, uncovered, for 12–15 minutes, turning the dumplings occasionally. Drain well and serve hot with a little melted butter poured over top.

Marinate sauerbraten in red wine, vinegar and vegetables for 2–3 days; braise and serve with potato dumplings

For chicken saté, pieces of the boned breast are marinated, then threaded on bamboo skewers and broiled over charcoal

Quick Marinade
for Broiled Steaks, Fish, and Meat for a Terrine

1 tablespoon finely chopped or sliced onion
3–4 tablespoons olive oil
2 teaspoons lemon juice, or wine vinegar
black pepper, freshly ground
3–4 tablespoons Madeira or sherry (for steak marinade only)

This quantity is enough for 4 steaks or fish fillets.

Method
Lay the meat or fish in a dish and sprinkle over the ingredients, including a generous amount of black pepper. Leave 2–3 hours before cooking.

Piquant Marinade
for Beef Steaks

1 cup tomato juice
$\frac{1}{4}$ cup olive oil
$\frac{1}{2}$ green bell pepper, cored, seeded and finely chopped
$\frac{1}{2}$ red bell pepper, cored, seeded and finely chopped
2 cloves of garlic, crushed
1 teaspoon chili powder
1 teaspoon Worcestershire sauce

This quantity is enough for 4 steaks.

Method
Combine all the ingredients in a saucepan, bring to a boil and simmer 10 minutes. Cool and pour over steaks. Cover and refrigerate for 2–3 hours, turning the meat once or twice. Drain and pat the steaks dry with paper towels before broiling.

Spiced Marinade
for Lamb Chops and Kebabs

$\frac{1}{2}$ teaspoon ground ginger
$\frac{1}{2}$ teaspoon ground turmeric
$\frac{1}{2}$ teaspoon ground allspice
$\frac{1}{2}$ teaspoon curry powder
clove of garlic, crushed
1 teaspoon lemon juice
6 tablespoons yogurt or sour cream

This quantity is enough for 4 large chops or kebabs.

Method
Combine the ingredients and brush or toss the meat with the mixture. Refrigerate for 2–3 hours before broiling.

Saté Marinade
for Chicken or Pork Saté

1 teaspoon ground caraway
1 teaspoon ground coriander
clove of garlic, crushed
1 tablespoon dark brown sugar
2 tablespoons soy sauce
1 tablespoon lemon juice
salt and pepper

This quantity is enough to marinate 3 boned breasts of chicken or $1\frac{1}{2}$ lb lean pork, cut into 1 inch pieces. Saté is the spicy kebab dish traditionally served on bamboo skewers throughout Indonesia.

Method
Combine the ingredients for the marinade with salt and pepper to taste. Toss the pork or chicken in the marinade; marinate 1–2 hours in the refrigerator. Thread the pieces on bamboo skewers and broil or barbecue.

Marinade for Game

2 cloves of garlic, peeled
2 medium onions, thinly sliced
2 medium carrots, thinly sliced
2 stalks of celery, thinly sliced (optional)
10–12 peppercorns
3 tablespoons olive oil
1½ cups red wine (a Burgundy or any robust red wine)
3 tablespoons red wine vinegar
3 strips of lemon rind
8 allspice or juniper berries, crushed

Method

Prepare as for beef marinade. Rich dark meat like venison needs extra sharpness, but seasoning and spices given here can be altered to taste. This recipe is also very good for pork.

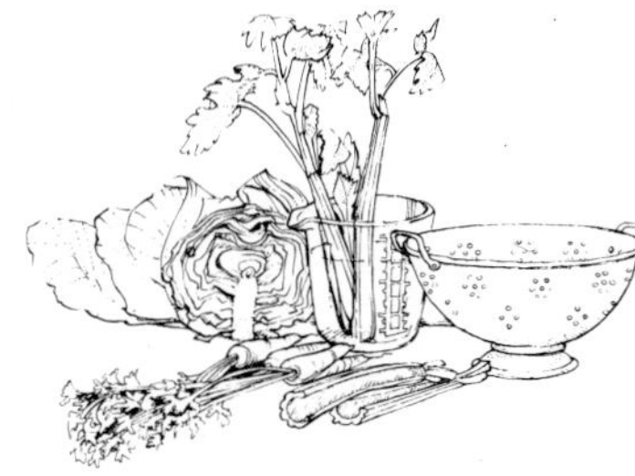

Braised Loin of Pork with Chestnuts

3–3½ lb loin of pork, boned and rolled
marinade for game

For braising
2 tablespoons oil
1 onion, sliced
1 carrot, sliced
bouquet garni
½ cup stock

For sauce
kneaded butter (made with 2 tablespoons butter and 1 tablespoon flour)
¾ cup sour cream
salt and pepper

For braised chestnuts
1½ lb chestnuts
1 tablespoon oil
1 onion, finely sliced
2 cups jellied stock

The spiciness of the game marinade used in this recipe is an excellent complement to the richness of pork.

Method

Pour the marinade over the pork, leaving the vegetables on top, and leave 1–2 days in the refrigerator, turning occasionally. Drain the meat and pat it dry with paper towels.

In a deep flameproof casserole, heat the oil and brown the meat on all sides. Take it out, add the onion and carrot and fry them over gentle heat, covered, for 5–7 minutes. Put back the pork, add bouquet garni and stock and pour over the marinade. Cover the pan and braise in a moderately low oven (325°F) for 2–2½ hours or until the pork is very tender. Start braising the chestnuts about an hour before the end of the pork braising time.

To braise chestnuts: prick the shell of each nut with a knife. Put the nuts in a pan of cold water, bring to a boil, then take from heat and peel while still hot, taking off the outer and inner skins.

In another flameproof casserole, heat oil, add onion and cook gently until soft. Spread the chestnuts on top, pour over the stock, add seasoning, cover the pot and braise in heated oven for 45 minutes or until the chestnuts are tender. Remove the lid from the pot and boil rapidly to reduce the liquid until almost all of it has evaporated and the chestnuts are glazed and shiny.

Take out the meat, slice, arrange on a platter and keep warm.

Strain the gravy and skim off fat. Bring the gravy to a boil and thicken it by whisking in the kneaded butter, a little at a time, until the sauce is the consistency of heavy cream. Take from the heat, stir in the sour cream and season to taste. Reheat the sauce carefully without boiling, spoon a little over the meat and serve the rest separately with the pork and braised chestnuts.

Kneaded Butter (Beurre Manié)

This is a liaison of twice as much butter as flour worked together as a paste on a plate with a fork and added in small pieces to thicken a mixture or liquid (usually at the end of the cooking process).

Braised Red Cabbage

1 medium head of red cabbage, shredded
2 tablespoons butter
1 onion, sliced
2 tart apples, pared, cored and sliced
2–3 tablespoons wine vinegar
1½ tablespoons sugar
salt and pepper
2–3 tablespoons water
kneaded butter, made with 2 tablespoons butter and 1 tablespoon flour

Braised cabbage is even better cooked the day before and reheated thoroughly just before serving.

Method

Blanch the cabbage in a kettle of boiling water for 1 minute; drain. The cabbage will turn deep violet at this point but when the vinegar is added it will return to its original color.

In a flameproof casserole melt the butter and fry the onion until soft but not browned. Add the apples, continue cooking 2–3 minutes and remove from the pan. Add the cabbage in layers with the apple mixture, sprinkling the layers with vinegar, sugar, salt and pepper and water. Cover with buttered brown paper and the lid and braise in a moderately low oven (325°F) for 1½–2 hours or until the cabbage is very tender. Stir the cabbage occasionally and moisten with a little extra water if necessary.

Stir in the kneaded butter a little at a time, adding just enough to thicken the cabbage juices slightly. Adjust seasoning.

Braised venison is garnished with glazed onions and decorated with a border of piped mashed potato

Braised Venison

3–4 lb roast of venison
marinade for game
thinly peeled rind of 1 orange and 1 lemon
kneaded butter, made with 2 tablespoons butter and 1 tablespoon flour
1 tablespoon red currant jelly
mashed potatoes for serving
2–3 tablespoons heavy cream (optional)

For braising
2 tablespoons oil or meat drippings
2 onions, diced
2 carrots, diced
2 stalks of celery, diced
bouquet garni
1½ cups jellied stock
salt and pepper

Venison is the meat of deer, and buck rather than doe meat is considered the best. Venison has no natural outer layer of fat, so it tends to lack succulence and tenderness and is usually marinated before cooking. The best cuts are from the haunch.

Method

Put the meat in a deep bowl; pour over the marinade, leaving the vegetables on top. Add the orange and lemon rinds, cover and refrigerate 2–3 days, turning the meat occasionally. Take the meat from the marinade and pat dry with paper towels.

In a deep flameproof casserole, heat the oil or drippings and brown the meat on all sides. Take out, add onions, carrots and celery, cover and cook gently for 5–7 minutes. Replace the venison and add bouquet garni with the stock, strained marinade and seasoning. Bring the mixture to a boil; cover pot with foil, then with the lid and braise in a moderately low oven (325°F) for 2–3 hours or until venison is very tender. Remove the venison and keep warm.

Strain the gravy, skim off fat, bring to a boil and whisk in kneaded butter a little at a time until the gravy is the consistency of heavy cream. Add the red currant jelly, stir until melted and taste for seasoning.

Arrange the venison on a platter and spoon over the sauce. Pipe a border of mashed potato around the platter just before serving.

If you like, add 2–3 tablespoons cream to the sauce just before serving. Serve the venison with braised celery or braised red cabbage, and red currant jelly separately.

Mashed Potatoes for Piping

Boil the potatoes, drain and dry them well on paper towels. Mash or put them through a sieve.

Gradually beat in boiling milk, allowing 1 cup for every 4 medium potatoes, with about 2 tablespoons butter, and season to taste. The potatoes can be kept hot up to 20 minutes by pouring 2–3 tablespoons hot milk over the leveled surface in the pan and then covering with the pan lid.

Beat the potatoes again before filling into a pastry bag for piping.

Braised Celery

bunch of celery
1 large onion, diced
1 large carrot, diced
2 tablespoons butter
½ cup jellied stock
salt and pepper
bouquet garni

Method

Wash the celery and slice off some of the leaves. Split the bunch in four and blanch in boiling salted water; drain.

In a large flameproof casserole sweat the onion and carrot in butter by covering the pot tightly with foil and the lid and cooking over very low heat until the vegetables are soft but not brown.

Put the celery, stock, salt, pepper and the bouquet garni in with the vegetables. Cover and braise for 1–1½ hours or until tender in a moderately low oven (325°F), basting from time to time. When cooked, the sauce should be well reduced and the celery glazed. Strain the sauce and pour over the celery in a vegetable dish.

Curried chicken may be served with cucumber raita, brinjal bhartha (at left), boiled rice and brinjal sambal (recipes on pages 77–79)

CREATE A COLORFUL CURRY FOR YOUR GUESTS

Take a look towards India and serve a curry with all the trimmings. There's a choice of curried chicken (you can tone it up or down to suit your taste) or a mild lamb curry with scallions. Serve one or both, as you prefer, but be generous with the accompaniments.

With such an authoritative flavor as Indian-style curry, wine seems out of the question. What's called for is something long and cooling. For the most part, the people of the great Indian sub-continent abstain from alcohol on religious grounds and drink tea instead. One might, therefore, accompany these dishes with iced tea and be entirely satisfied. Most Americans, however, will appreciate a cold mug of lager beer with these hot dishes, as they do with foods of the American Southwest.

Curried Chicken

or

Methee Bhaji (Mild Lamb Curry)

Boiled Rice

Okra Foogath *Cucumber Raita*

Brinjal Sambal *Brinjal Bhartha*

Masur Dahl (Lentil Purée)

Fresh Chutney

Macédoine of Fresh Fruits

Tuiles aux Amandes
(Almond Cookies)

Beer

TIMETABLE

Day before
Make almond cookies and store in airtight container.
Make fresh chutney, brinjal sambal and bhartha, raita and okra foogath and store in covered containers in refrigerator.

Morning
Cook chicken curry and place in casserole ready for reheating. Cook lamb curry and put in casserole for reheating.
Prepare fruit macédoine.
Cook rice: when thoroughly dry put in buttered dish ready for reheating.
Cook lentils for masur dahl and beat until a purée. Cover and keep in a cool place.
Assemble equipment for final cooking from 7:00 for dinner around 8 p.m.

You will find that **cooking times** given in the individual recipes for these dishes have sometimes been adapted in the timetable to help you when cooking and serving this menu as a party meal.

Order of Work

7:00
Set oven at moderate (350°F).
Transfer fruit macédoine, almond cookies and the cold accompaniments for the curry to the serving dishes.

7:15
Put curried chicken and lamb curry casseroles in the oven to reheat.

7:30
Put rice in the oven to reheat.
Finish cooking the masur dahl.

7:45
Reduce oven heat to warm and keep the prepared dishes warm.
Reheat the okra foogath and chutney, if serving hot, for the curry. This will take only a few minutes on top of stove.

8:00
Serve dinner.

Quantities for Serving
The two curries together will serve 4 people generously. If you prefer to serve either one or the other separately, double the lamb curry recipe or make the chicken curry with a larger chicken.

Rice should always be served with a curry, and the more accompaniments the better. Here we give recipes for okra foogath, cucumber raita, brinjal sambal, brinjal bhartha, masur dahl and fresh chutney.

Entrée

Curried Chicken

3–3½ lb frying or roasting chicken
2 tablespoons oil
2 onions, chopped
1 tablespoon ground coriander
1 teaspoon ground cumin
1 tablespoon chili powder (or to taste)
½ teaspoon turmeric
1 cup boiling water
2 tablespoons grated fresh or shredded unsweetened coconut, or 1–2 tablespoons ground almonds
salt
3 medium tomatoes, peeled, seeded and chopped

This Indian recipe is very hot and the quantity of chili powder can be reduced to taste. The dish can be kept hot easily, or can be prepared in advance and reheated.

Method
Cut the chicken into pieces and sauté them in the oil in a shallow pan until brown. Remove the chicken, add the onions and cook slowly until golden. Mix spices together, add them to the pan and continue cooking 1–2 minutes.

Pour the boiling water on the coconut or almonds and leave to infuse for 10 minutes; strain, pressing well to extract all the liquid, add this liquid to the pan and bring just to a boil. Replace chicken pieces in the pan, add a little salt and simmer, covered, for 15–20 minutes.

Add tomatoes and continue cooking 15 minutes or until the chicken is tender; taste for seasoning.

Serve with boiled rice and the vegetable accompaniments of your choice.

Alternative entrée

Methee Bhaji
(Mild Lamb Curry)

1½ lb boneless leg or lean shoulder of lamb, cut into 1 inch cubes
1 large onion, finely chopped
clove of garlic, finely chopped
2 tablespoons butter
2 tablespoons oil
1 tablespoon curry powder
1 teaspoon allspice
½ teaspoon turmeric
½ teaspoon freshly ground black pepper
¼ teaspoon nutmeg
1 tablespoon tomato paste, or 2–3 fresh tomatoes, peeled, seeded and chopped
4 scallions, chopped
little stock, or water (optional)
salt
squeeze of lemon juice or to taste

Method
In a skillet, fry the onion and garlic in butter and oil for 3–4 minutes until soft. Mix the curry powder and spices together, add them to the pan, cook 2 minutes, then add the tomato paste or fresh tomatoes and cubes of lamb. Stir well, cover the pan and cook over very low heat for 30–40 minutes.

Add the scallions and continue cooking about 15 minutes or until the meat is tender. If necessary, add a little stock or water while the curry is cooking to prevent it from becoming dry – the finished dish should be rich and thick in consistency.

Just before serving add salt and lemon juice to taste. Serve with rice, okra foogath or other accompaniments.

For chicken curry, first cut the chicken into pieces; then sauté in oil in a shallow pan

Okra Foogath

1 lb fresh okra
$\frac{1}{4}$ cup butter
1 onion, finely sliced
2 cloves of garlic, crushed
1 tablespoon finely chopped fresh ginger, or 2 teaspoons grated dry ginger
2–3 fresh chilis, seeded and finely chopped
$\frac{1}{2}$ teaspoon ground chili pepper
2–3 fresh tomatoes, peeled, seeded and thinly sliced
2 tablespoons grated fresh coconut, or 1 tablespoon shredded unsweetened coconut
salt

Method

Wash the okra, dry it well and trim the stems. Leave whole and place in a pan with $\frac{1}{4}$ inch water. Cover and cook 6–8 minutes or until the okra is tender. Drain well and set aside.

Heat the butter and fry the onion, garlic, ginger chopped chilis and chili pepper for 3–4 minutes. Add the tomato slices and coconut and simmer 3–4 minutes longer. Add the okra with salt to taste and simmer gently 2 minutes or until heated.

Okra is a small prolific plant of the mallow family that grows in South America and the southern U.S. Sometimes called gumbo, okra is an essential part of the traditional New Orleans dish, gumbo.

Ripe okra seeds produce an oil that is used in Mediterranean countries. The seeds may also be ground as a coffee substitute.

Okra is at its peak June through August, and varies from the short, smooth whitish-green variety to the long, thin, ridged green kind.

Accompaniments to entrées

Boiled Rice

Allow $\frac{1}{4}$ cup rice per person and boil at least 3 quarts water for every cup of rice. Add salt and slice of lemon to give flavor and whiteness. Sprinkle in the rice, stir with a fork to prevent sticking and boil steadily for 12–15 minutes or until rice is just tender.

To stop the rice cooking, tip at once into a colander and drain. Rinse thoroughly with hot running water to wash away any remaining starch, making several draining holes in the rice with the handle of a wooden spoon. Transfer rice to a large tray or platter, spread it out and stand in a warm place or in a very low oven to dry for at least 15 minutes before serving, turning occasionally with a fork.

For easy reheating, spoon rice into a well-buttered, shallow ovenproof dish, cover with buttered foil and heat in a moderate oven (350°F) for about 30 minutes. Serve rice from the dish in which it was reheated.

For this chicken curry, brown the pieces before adding spices and tomatoes. Serve with boiled rice and accompaniments of your choic

Accompaniments to entrée

Cucumber Raita

2 cucumbers
salt
$\frac{3}{4}$ cup plain yogurt
black pepper, freshly ground
sugar (to taste)

Method
Peel the cucumbers, cut in half lengthwise, discard the seeds and grate the flesh coarsely. Sprinkle with salt, cover and refrigerate for about 30 minutes. Then rinse with cold water, drain well and mix with the yogurt, black pepper and sugar to taste.

Brinjal Sambal

1 medium eggplant
2 onions
3 green chilis, or 1 green bell pepper, cored, seeded and finely chopped
salt
sugar (to taste)
juice of 1 lemon
1 lime or lemon sliced

Green chilis make the brinjals hot and green pepper makes them sweet.

Method
Wrap the eggplant in foil and bake in a moderate oven (350°F) for 30–40 minutes, or until it is tender when pierced with a fork. Peel the eggplant and crush the flesh. Mix the pulp with 1 onion, grated or finely chopped, chilis or green pepper, salt and sugar to taste and lemon juice to sharpen the flavor.

Chill the mixture, transfer to a serving dish and garnish the top with the second onion, thinly sliced and pushed into rings, and slices of lime or lemon.

Brinjal Bhartha

1 large eggplant, squash or cucumber
2 green chilis, cored, seeded and finely chopped
1 tablespoon oil
2 tablespoons very finely chopped onion
$\frac{1}{2}$ teaspoon cumin seeds
salt
pinch of sugar
squeeze of lemon juice (optional)

Method
Set the oven at moderate (350°F).

Rub the eggplant, squash or cucumber with oil and bake in heated oven for 1 hour or until soft. Scoop out the flesh and mash well, discarding the skin. Add onion, cumin seeds, chilis, remaining oil and salt and sugar to taste. A squeeze of lemon juice may be needed to sharpen the flavor.

Fresh Chutney

1 medium tart apple
1 small onion
2 tomatoes, peeled, seeded and chopped
clove of garlic, crushed with 1 teaspoon salt
1 slice of canned pimiento, chopped
3 tablespoons chopped celery
1 tablespoon chopped mint
1 tablespoon grated fresh horseradish or 2 tablespoons prepared horseradish
1 tablespoon sugar
2 tablespoons wine vinegar

Method
Pare and core the tart apple and work it through a food mill with the onion. Combine all ingredients in a saucepan and cook, stirring, for 2–3 minutes. Serve chutney hot or cold.

Further Accompaniments for Curry
Grated fresh coconut, or shredded unsweetened coconut
Mango chutney
Peanuts
Preserved kumquats
Crumbled crisply fried bacon

Masur Dahl
(Lentil Purée)

1 cup Egyptian lentils, soaked overnight and drained
$2\frac{1}{2}$–3 cups stock
$\frac{1}{2}$ teaspoon ground red chili pepper
$\frac{1}{2}$ teaspoon turmeric
salt
2 tablespoons oil
1 small onion, finely chopped
$\frac{1}{2}$ teaspoon chopped fresh ginger root
$\frac{1}{4}$ teaspoon ground cinnamon
$\frac{1}{4}$ teaspoon ground cloves
$\frac{1}{2}$ teaspoon ground coriander

Method
Put the drained lentils in a saucepan with $2\frac{1}{2}$ cups stock, the chili pepper and turmeric. Cover, bring to a boil and simmer $1–1\frac{1}{2}$ hours or until the lentils are very soft. Beat them with a whisk or a wooden spoon until the mixture is a purée, adding a little salt and more stock if necessary – the consistency should be soft and smooth, not sticky or soupy.

In a skillet heat the oil, add the onion and cook until golden brown. Stir in the ginger and other spices and cook, stirring, for 2–3 minutes. Combine with the lentil purée and taste for seasoning.

Macédoine of Fresh Fruits

2 oranges
2 tangerines
3 ripe pears
½ lb green or black grapes
3 bananas
2–3 tablespoons kirsch or Maraschino liqueur (optional)
¾ cup heavy cream, stiffly whipped (for serving) – optional

For sugar syrup
6 tablespoons sugar
6 tablespoons water
strip of lemon rind, or piece of vanilla bean

Method

To prepare the sugar syrup: heat the sugar in the water, add lemon rind or vanilla bean, and boil 1 minute. Pour into a bowl and let cool. Remove lemon rind or vanilla bean.

Cut the rind and white pith from the oranges with a sharp, serrated-edge knife, then cut between each membrane to remove the sections. Peel and slice the tangerines across the sections, discarding all seeds. Pare and quarter the pears, remove the cores and cut each quarter in half. Remove the grape seeds. Peel the bananas and cut them into thick diagonal slices.

Moisten the mixture of fruit with sugar syrup, add the liqueur, if used, and turn the fruit over carefully with a spoon. Cover the bowl with a plate or plastic wrap and refrigerate for at least 1 hour to draw out the juices of the fruit. Serve with whipped cream, if you like, and almond cookies.

Curl baked tuiles or almond cookies around a rolling pin. If you let them cool they will break as you shape them

To prepare grapes: scoop out seeds with the eye of a trussing needle or stick the ends of a bobby pin in a cork, sterilize curved end in an open flame and use this makeshift tool.

Accompaniment to dessert

Tuiles aux Amandes
(Almond Cookies)

¾ cup finely slivered almonds
6 tablespoons butter
6 tablespoons sugar
½ cup flour
pinch of salt

These cookies are known as 'tuiles' because they resemble curved tiles.

Method

Set oven at hot (400°F).

In a bowl cream the butter until soft and gradually work in the sugar until the mixture is light and fluffy. Sift the flour with the salt and stir it into the mixture with the almonds. Drop the mixture, a teaspoon at a time, onto a well-greased baking sheet and flatten each cookie with a fork dipped in cold water.

Watchpoint: leave plenty of space between the cookies as they spread during baking.

Bake cookies in heated oven for 6–8 minutes or until they are lightly browned. Let them stand 1–2 seconds before removing them from the baking sheet with a thin metal spatula. Immediately shape them around a rolling pin and leave until firm. If the last cookies on the baking sheet are too cool to shape, return them to the oven for 1–2 minutes.

When the cookies are cold and firm, store in an airtight container.

Macédoine of fresh fruits is served with almond cookies

COOKING WITH PASTA (I)

All pasta is made of a flour and water dough – the proportions may vary, and eggs are often added for richness, but the dough remains basically a pliable flour and water mixture that is kneaded and worked into an astonishing variety of shapes. For good quality pasta, semolina flour is used, although it is possible to make a dough with regular flour.

All pasta must be given a preliminary cooking in water or stock before it is tossed with butter or a sauce, or stuffed or layered with sauce and baked in the oven. The only exception is the tiny pasta for soup which is cooked in the soup itself.

The better the pasta, the simpler the treatment it needs. Few pasta dishes can rival the famous noodles Alfredo made with fresh egg noodles, cream, butter and Parmesan cheese. The quality of the ingredients makes all the difference to pasta dishes; be sure to use freshly grated Parmesan cheese and grind black pepper from the mill to produce the finest flavor.

Preliminary Cooking

This is always the same (unless the pasta is added to soup). Bring a large pan of salted water to a boil – there should be enough water so the pasta does not stick together (at least 2–3 quarts for $\frac{1}{2}$ lb pasta). Lower the pasta into it – long varieties like spaghetti will soften quickly so they can be curled into the pan. Bring the water back to a boil, stir the pasta with a fork to separate the pieces and to prevent them from sticking to the bottom of the pan, lower the heat and simmer 8–12 minutes, depending on the shape of the pasta, stirring occasionally. For example, spaghetti and noodles take 8–10 minutes to cook, and macaroni 10–12 minutes. Stock is sometimes used for the preliminary cooking instead of water.

To test if the pasta is cooked, try a piece between your teeth. Perfectly cooked pasta should offer a perceptible resistance – known in Italy as 'al dente'; never let it cook until it is soft. Another test: when you can sever it with your thumbnail it is ready.

Strain the pasta at once into a colander and rinse it with hot water to wash away the starch. Tip it back into the saucepan, toss with butter and freshly ground black pepper and serve at once.

If the pasta must be kept hot for a short time, return it to the rinsed pan after draining, add a cup or two of hot water, cover the pan and keep in a warm place. This prevents the pasta from becoming sticky. Just before serving, drain the pasta again and finish as above.

Quantities of pasta for serving are very much a matter of appetite. When served as a side dish with meat or poultry, $\frac{1}{2}$ lb pasta is usually enough for 4 people. However, if the pasta is served as an entrée alone (with a sauce) as much as 1 lb may be needed for 4 people.

Semolina is the hard portion of wheat which remains after the flour, bran and chaff have been removed.

There are two types of semolina – one is made from regular wheat and used for puddings; the other comes from hard durum wheat and is used for all good quality homemade or commercial pasta.

Durum wheat semolina flour is particularly suitable for pasta because it contains a high proportion of protein that prevents the starch from breaking down during cooking. This produces a pasta that stays firm and resilient.

Note: a recipe for fresh ravioli dough is given on page 90, and recipes for fresh lasagne are included in Volume 8.

Macaroni and Cheese

$\frac{1}{2}$ lb macaroni
$\frac{1}{2}$ cup grated cheese
2 cups mornay sauce (see box)
little extra milk (optional)

Mornay sauce combines particularly well with the larger pasta like macaroni. The sauce can be tossed simply with the macaroni, or the sauce mixture can be placed on top of macaroni, sprinkled with grated cheese and baked to form a brown crust. A mixture of Gruyère and Parmesan cheese is ideal for the sauce; dry Cheddar is also suitable.

Method

Break the macaroni in half if it is long and cook 10–12 minutes until 'al dente'. Make mornay sauce and season well. Drain the macaroni, rinse with hot water, return to the pan and add the sauce. Stir gently to mix and transfer to a buttered gratin or ovenproof dish. Sprinkle the cheese on top and bake in a hot oven (400°F) for 15 minutes or until golden brown.

Watchpoint: there must be plenty of sauce for good macaroni and cheese. If the sauce seems thick after adding the cheese, thin it with a little extra milk.

Mornay Sauce

For 2 cup quantity: melt 3 tablespoons butter in a saucepan, remove from heat and stir in 2 tablespoons flour. Pour on 1 cup milk, blend until smooth with whisk or wooden spoon. Add another 1 cup milk, season lightly with salt and pepper, and bring to a boil, stirring continuously. Simmer 2 minutes, remove from heat and gradually stir in $\frac{1}{2}$ cup grated cheese, and a little dry mustard.

A good macaroni and cheese has plenty of mornay sauce; brown under the broiler just before serving

Conchiglie alla funghi (pasta shells with mushrooms) is sprinkled with parsley and Parmesan cheese for serving

Macaroni con Acciughe
(Macaroni with Anchovies)

¾ lb macaroni
12 anchovy fillets, soaked in a little milk to remove salt and drained and chopped
2 tablespoons olive oil
3 tablespoons chopped Italian parsley (fresh coriander)
clove of garlic, crushed
2 teaspoons capers, finely chopped
¼ cup Italian or Greek ripe olives, pitted and chopped
1 red or green bell pepper, cored, seeded and chopped
3 cups tomato sauce (see page 95)
salt
2 tablespoons butter
black pepper, freshly ground

Method
In a skillet heat the oil and fry the anchovies, parsley, garlic, capers, olives and bell pepper until very soft. Add the mixture to the tomato sauce and simmer 30–40 minutes, stirring occasionally, until the sauce is thick and well flavored. Taste for seasoning.

Cook the macaroni in plenty of boiling salted water for 10–12 minutes until 'al dente'. Drain and toss with butter, black pepper and half the sauce. Pile in a bowl and spoon over the remaining sauce.

Conchiglie all'Inferno

¾ lb conchiglie (pasta shells)
2 tablespoons olive oil
1 onion, chopped
2 cloves of garlic, crushed
2 lb Italian plum tomatoes, peeled, seeded and chopped, or 4 cups canned plum tomatoes
1 cup red wine
1 fresh red chili pepper, cored, seeded and chopped, or 1 teaspoon crushed red chili pepper
¼ cup tomato purée
salt
2 tablespoons butter
½ cup freshly grated Parmesan cheese (to serve)

For this 'hot as hell' dish you may use more or less chili pepper, according to taste. The sauce improves if left a day or two to mellow.

Method
In a saucepan heat the oil and sauté the onion and garlic until brown. Add the tomatoes, wine, pepper, tomato purée and salt to taste, and simmer over very low heat for 30 minutes or until the mixture is very thick, stirring occasionally.

Cook the conchiglie for 12–15 minutes until 'al dente' and drain. Toss with the butter, then with half the sauce Spoon the remaining sauce over and serve with Parmesan cheese.

Conchiglie alla Funghi
(Pasta Shells with Mushrooms)

¾ lb conchiglie (pasta shells)
½ lb fresh button mushrooms or 1 cup dried mushrooms
2 tablespoons oil
1 onion, chopped
½ lb ground beef
½ lb ground pork
2 cloves of garlic, crushed
1 cup red wine
½ teaspoon thyme
salt and pepper
2 tablespoons butter

For serving
1 tablespoon chopped Italian parsley (fresh coriander) – for sprinkling
½ cup freshly grated Parmesan cheese
¼ lb thinly sliced pepperoni or salami sausage

Method
Peel and wipe the fresh mushrooms or soak the dried mushrooms in warm water to cover for 30 minutes and drain; chop them.

In a saucepan heat the oil and fry the onion until soft. Stir in the beef and pork and cook, stirring, until brown add the garlic, wine, chopped mushrooms, thyme, salt and pepper and simmer, stirring occasionally, for 30–40 minutes or until the mixture is well reduced and thick.

Cook conchiglie in plenty of boiling salted water for 12–15 minutes until 'al dente' and drain. Toss with the butter and pile in a serving dish. Spoon the sauce in the center, sprinkle with chopped parsley and a little grated Parmesan cheese and serve the remaining cheese separately. Arrange the sausage around the edge of the dish or serve it separately.

Farfalle con Piselli

¾ lb farfalle (pasta bows)
1½ cups cooked peas
¼ cup butter
bunch of scallions, trimmed and cut in 1 inch lengths
2 tablespoons chopped parsley
salt
black pepper, freshly ground

Method
Cook the farfalle for 10–12 minutes until 'al dente' and drain.

In a skillet melt the butter and sauté the scallions until soft. Add the peas and heat thoroughly. Toss with the cooked farfalle and parsley, adding salt and plenty of freshly ground pepper.

Spaghetti alla Carbonara

1 lb spaghetti
1 medium onion, thinly sliced
8 slices of bacon, diced
1 tablespoon oil
½ cup white wine
4 eggs
1 cup freshly grated Parmesan cheese
2 tablespoons chopped parsley
black pepper, freshly ground
3 tablespoons butter

Method

Fry the onion and bacon in the oil until brown and pour off the excess fat. Add the wine and simmer until it has almost evaporated.

Beat the eggs with the cheese, parsley and plenty of pepper until smooth.

Cook spaghetti 8–10 minutes until 'al dente' and drain. Return to the pan with the butter, add the egg mixture with bacon and onion and toss quickly over low heat until the egg thickens creamily. Remove from the heat and serve at once.

Tomatoes for Pasta

Fresh Italian-type plum tomatoes are ideal for pasta as they have a rich mellow flavor. If they are not available, canned plum tomatoes are the best substitute unless you can find fresh garden tomatoes that are ripe and full of juice.

If you do use regular or garden tomatoes, strengthen the color and flavor by adding 1–2 tablespoons of tomato paste or ½ cup tomato purée.

Linguine Tutto Mare

¾ lb linguine
12 hard-shell clams, washed, or 6 clams and 6 mussels, scrubbed
4 baby squid, cleaned
12 medium uncooked, peeled shrimps
6 tablespoons olive oil
1 clove of garlic, peeled
1½ lb Italian plum tomatoes, peeled, seeded and chopped, or 3 cups canned plum tomatoes
1 tablespoon chopped parsley
pinch of rosemary
salt
black pepper, freshly ground

Method

Heat the oil in a saucepan, add the whole garlic, sauté until golden and discard it. Add tomatoes, parsley, rosemary and salt and pepper to taste and simmer, uncovered, for 20 minutes or until the mixture is thick and pulpy.

Put the clams and mussels in a large pan, cover and cook over high heat until the shells open, stirring once. Discard any that do not open. Remove the clams and mussels from their shells and add to the tomato mixture, with their juice (strained through cheesecloth).

Cut the squid into medium-sized pieces and add to the tomato mixture. Simmer 10 minutes, add the shrimps and simmer 5 minutes longer.

Cook the linguine 8–10 minutes until 'al dente' and drain. Toss with half the seafood mixture and spoon the remainder over the linguine before serving.

Tagliatelle con Pepperoni

¾ lb tagliatelle or egg noodles
1 lb pepperoni sausage
2 onions, chopped
1 small head of green cabbage, shredded
salt
black pepper, freshly ground

Method

Remove the casing from the pepperoni and break or cut the sausage into pieces.

In a flameproof casserole fry the pepperoni until the fat runs, add the onion and continue cooking until the onion and sausage are brown. Pour off most of the fat, add the cabbage with salt and pepper to taste, cover the pan and cook over low heat, or bake in a moderate oven (350°F) for 20–30 minutes or until the cabbage is tender.

Cook the tagliatelle or noodles for 10–12 minutes until 'al dente', drain and toss with the sausage mixture.

Manicotti con Fegato
(Manicotti with Chicken Liver)

¾ lb manicotti
1 cup chicken livers, chopped
2 tablespoons butter
1 onion, finely chopped
2 cups (½ lb) finely chopped mushrooms
salt
black pepper, freshly ground
½ cup white wine
1 tablespoon chopped parsley
¼ cup freshly grated Parmesan cheese (to serve)

Method

In a skillet, melt the butter and sauté the onion until soft. Add the chopped mushrooms and chicken livers with salt and pepper to taste and sauté, stirring, for 3–4 minutes until the livers are brown. Add the wine and simmer until the mixture is fairly thick. Stir in the parsley.

Cook manicotti 12–15 minutes until 'al dente' and drain. Toss with the liver and mushroom mixture, sprinkle with Parmesan cheese and serve.

Fettucine con Prosciutto

1 lb fettucine
¼ lb sliced prosciutto, chopped
¼ cup olive oil
1 onion, chopped
1 cup white wine
1 lb Italian plum tomatoes, peeled, seeded and chopped, or 2 cups canned plum tomatoes
2 teaspoons basil
1 tablespoon chopped parsley
salt
black pepper, freshly ground
1 cup (¼ lb) sliced mushrooms
½ cup freshly grated Parmesan cheese (to serve)

Method

In a saucepan heat the oil and fry the onion until soft. Add the prosciutto and cook 1 minute. Add the wine, tomatoes, basil, parsley and salt and pepper to taste and simmer the mixture 15 minutes or until thick. Stir in the mushrooms and simmer 10 minutes longer.

Cook the fettucine 8–10 minutes until 'al dente' and drain. Toss with the prosciutto, mushroom and tomato mixture, sprinkle with cheese and serve.

Fettucine Alfredo

1 lb fettucine
1 cup unsalted butter, softened
1 cup freshly grated Parmesan cheese
$\frac{1}{2}$ cup heavy cream
black pepper, freshly ground

Method

Cook the fettucine 8–10 minutes in boiling, salted water until 'al dente' and drain.

Heat the butter in a saucepan until creamy, add the noodles and toss, off the heat. Add the cheese and toss again over low heat. Add the cream and continue tossing until the mixture is very hot. Sprinkle with black pepper and serve at once.

Rigatoni con Quattro Formaggi

1 lb rigatoni

For filling
1 lb ricotta cheese or 1 lb creamed cottage cheese
$\frac{1}{2}$ cup grated Parmesan cheese
$\frac{1}{2}$ cup grated Pecorino cheese
$\frac{3}{4}$ cup ($\frac{1}{4}$ lb) diced Mozzarella cheese
$\frac{1}{4}$ cup chopped walnuts
2 eggs, beaten to mix
2 tablespoons chopped parsley
salt
black pepper, freshly ground

For sauce
6 tablespoons butter
1 cup ($\frac{1}{4}$ lb) sliced mushrooms
5 tablespoons flour
4 cups milk
pinch of nutmeg
1 cup freshly grated Parmesan cheese

Serves 6 people.

Method

Cook rigatoni 12–15 minutes until 'al dente' and drain.

To make the filling: soften the ricotta or cottage cheese and stir in the remaining ingredients with plenty of salt and pepper. With a teaspoon, fill the rigatoni and arrange them in a buttered baking dish.

To make the sauce: in a pan melt the butter and sauté the mushrooms until tender. Stir in the flour off the heat, pour in the milk and bring to a boil, stirring. Season with nutmeg, and salt and pepper and simmer 2 minutes. Take from heat, stir in most of the Parmesan cheese and spoon over the rigatoni.

Sprinkle the top with the remaining Parmesan and bake in a hot oven (400°F) for 15 minutes or until brown.

Rigatoni con quattro formaggi is made with ricotta or creamed cottage cheese, grated Parmesan, Pecorino and Mozzarella cheeses

Ravioli

Freshly made ravioli, usually filled with a meat mixture, can be bought in some Italian specialty stores.

However, if you want to serve a superb ravioli but cannot buy it freshly made, it is well worth making your own by using the following recipe. You must prepare this well before cooking time to allow 2–3 hours for the dough to dry once it has been filled. Choose and make your filling while the dough is left 20–30 minutes to relax and lose its elasticity.

To Cook Ravioli

Simmer the ravioli in stock or water for 15–20 minutes or until the pasta is 'al dente'. Drain and lay the ravioli in a buttered baking dish. Coat with tomato sauce and bake in a moderate oven (350°F) for 15 minutes or until very hot. Serve sprinkled with freshly grated Parmesan cheese.

Ravioli Dough

2 cups semolina or regular flour
$\frac{1}{2}$ teaspoon salt
$1\frac{1}{2}$ tablespoons olive oil
2 eggs, beaten to mix
3–4 tablespoons milk or water

Ravioli cutter or pastry wheel

If using regular flour, $1–1\frac{1}{2}$ more tablespoons milk or water will be needed.

Method

Sift the flour with the salt onto a board or Formica-type surface, make a well in the center and add the oil, eggs and half the milk or water.

Roll out half of the ravioli dough until it is paper thin

Spoon the cooked spinach and ricotta filling onto dough

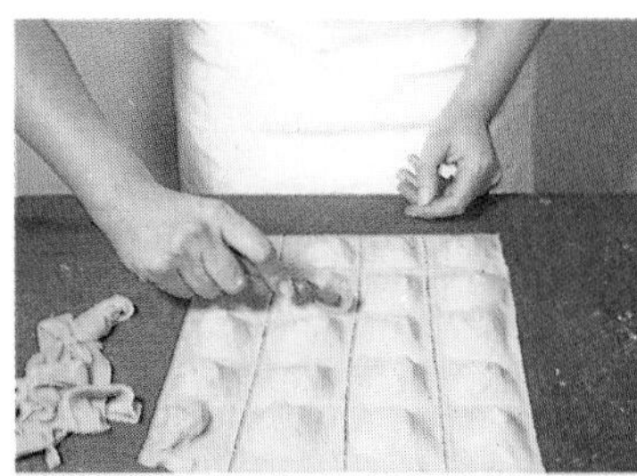

With a pastry wheel, cut the filled ravioli into squares

Start mixing the oil, eggs and water together, gradually drawing in the flour and adding more liquid as it is needed. Work the dough until it is smooth and firm – it should be fairly soft but not sticky. Cover with a cloth and leave 20–30 minutes so the dough relaxes and loses any elasticity.

Cut it in half and roll out one half until it is paper thin. Slide it to one side and roll out the second piece, also paper thin. Brush the dough with water and place the chosen filling, one teaspoon at a time, at regular intervals on one piece of dough. Lift and lay the other piece on top and, with a small ball of dough, press the top piece down to seal around each little mound of filling.

Stamp out each one with a fluted ravioli cutter or cut in squares with a pastry wheel. Leave 2–3 hours to dry a little, then cook as described left.

Fillings for Ravioli

Savory Meat

1 cup ground cooked chicken, or ham
2 tablespoons thick béchamel sauce (enough to bind the meat), or tomato sauce (see page 95)
1 tablespoon chopped parsley, or mixed herbs (basil, chives, thyme)
1 egg yolk

Method

Mix all the ingredients together and season well. The mixture should be firm and quite stiff.

Cheese

$\frac{3}{4}$ cup (6 oz) ricotta or creamed cottage cheese
$\frac{1}{2}$ cup grated Parmesan cheese
black pepper, freshly ground
2 tablespoons finely chopped parsley
salt

Method

Combine all the ingredients and season well. Fill ravioli dough as above.

Spinach and Ricotta

1 package frozen chopped spinach or $\frac{1}{2}–\frac{3}{4}$ lb fresh spinach
$\frac{1}{4}$ cup ricotta cheese or creamed cottage cheese
small pinch of ground mace or nutmeg
salt and pepper

Method

If using frozen spinach, cook according to the package directions and drain well. If using fresh spinach, cook it for 5 minutes in boiling salted water, drain thoroughly and work through a sieve or chop finely; let cool.

Work the cheese through a sieve and mix in the cold spinach. Add the spice and season well with salt and pepper. The mixture should be a firm purée.

Ravioli in Consommé

Parboil homemade ravioli (see left) in plenty of simmering salted water for 10 minutes and drain. Add the ravioli to 4 cups beef or chicken stock or consommé and simmer 5–10 minutes longer until the ravioli is 'al dente'.

Serve ravioli in soup bowls, with grated cheese separately.

Pasta (1)

Ravioli in consommé – the filled pasta shapes are poached in the consommé

Tortellini (stuffed pasta turnovers) are served in a cream sauce; tortellini at left are dried not fresh

Tortellini

Tortellini are made with the same dough as ravioli. They are little, stuffed turnovers with the ends pulled around to form a circle. They can be filled with any of the same fillings as ravioli and are available dried in some specialty Italian stores.

To Make Tortellini

Make ravioli dough as described on page 90 and roll it out very thinly.

Cut out 2–2½ inch rounds with a cookie cutter and put a teaspoon of the choosen filling in the center of each. Brush the edges of the dough with water, fold over to form a semicircle and press down the edges to seal firmly.

Bend the shapes, seam out, to form a circle and press the ends firmly together, moistening them with water. Let dry 2–3 hours.

Watchpoint: be sure to shape the circles before the dough starts to dry.

To Cook Tortellini

Simmer the tortellini in plenty of salted water for 15–20 minutes or until the pasta is 'al dente' – fresh tortellini cooks more quickly than dried. Drain.

Melt 2 tablespoons butter in a pan and add the tortellini. In a bowl beat 2 eggs with 1 cup heavy cream, add to the tortellini and toss over low heat until the sauce thickens creamily. Season with salt and freshly ground black pepper and serve at once with grated Parmesan cheese separately.

Canneloni

1 lb canneloni
3 cups tomato sauce (see page 95)
½ cup grated Parmesan cheese

For filling
1 lb ground raw veal or pork or mixture of both
1½ cups béchamel sauce (made with 3 tablespoons flour, 3 tablespoons butter, 1½ cups milk infused with slice of onion, bay leaf, blade of mace and 6 peppercorns)
2 egg yolks
pinch of ground mace or nutmeg
salt
black pepper, freshly ground

Pastry bag and a large plain tube

Canneloni may also be filled with the mixtures given for ravioli on page 90. Quantities given there should be doubled.

Method

To make the filling: make the béchamel sauce and cool thoroughly. Stir in the ground meat with the egg yolks, mace or nutmeg and salt and pepper to taste. The mixture should be stiff.

Cook the canneloni for 12–15 minutes until 'al dente', lift out carefully, dip in cold water and drain on paper towels. Put the filling into the pastry bag fitted with a large plain tube and pipe the filling into the canneloni.

Place canneloni in a shallow, buttered flameproof casserole and spoon over the tomato sauce (this should just cover them). Bring to a boil on top of the stove, cover and bake in a moderate oven (350°F) for 40–45 minutes. Take off the lid 10 minutes before the end of cooking time, sprinkle the casserole with grated cheese and increase the heat of the oven to hot (400°F) so the cheese browns.

If you prefer, the canneloni may simply be sprinkled with cheese before serving, instead of being browned.

SAUCES FOR PASTA

Quantities given in the following sauce recipes are enough to accompany 1 lb pasta.

Bolognese Sauce 1

1 tablespoon oil
¼ lb salt pork, diced
¼ lb raw ham, diced
1 onion, chopped
1 carrot, chopped
clove of garlic, crushed
¼ lb ground pork
¼ lb ground veal
1 lb ground beef
1 cup stock
½ cup red wine
½ lb Italian plum tomatoes, peeled, seeded and chopped, or 1 cup canned plum tomatoes
1 cup hot water
pinch of nutmeg
salt and pepper
1 cup (¼ lb) sliced mushrooms
½ cup chicken livers, chopped
½ cup freshly grated Parmesan cheese (to serve)

Serve this sauce on top of the cooked pasta in a broad band.

Method

In a large saucepan heat the oil and brown the salt pork. Add the ham, onion, carrot and garlic and cook until the vegetables are soft but not browned. Stir in the ground meats and cook the mixture, stirring, until the meats are browned. Add the stock and wine and simmer 5 minutes. Stir in the tomatoes, water, nutmeg and salt and pepper to taste, cover the pan and simmer for 1 hour or until the sauce is thick and rich, stirring occasionally to prevent it from sticking. Add the mushrooms and chicken livers, and simmer 10 minutes longer.

Taste the sauce for seasoning and spoon over cooked pasta. Serve freshly grated Parmesan cheese separately.

Bolognese Sauce 2

3 tablespoons oil
1 medium onion, chopped
1 lb ground beef
1 tablespoon tomato paste
1 clove of garlic, crushed
½ cup stock
½ cup red wine
pinch of nutmeg
salt and pepper
1 cup (¼ lb) chopped mushrooms

This simpler version of Bolognese sauce is often used with canneloni, or for layering lasagne (see Volume 8).

Method

In a saucepan, heat the oil and fry the onion until soft. Stir in the beef and cook, stirring, until brown. Add the tomato paste, garlic, stock, wine, nutmeg and salt and pepper to taste and simmer the sauce over very low heat, uncovered, for 20 minutes or until thick. Stir occasionally. Add the mushrooms, cook 10 minutes longer and serve.

Bolognese sauce is ideal for many pastas like farfalle (pasta bows) and pennini (small tubes) shown here

Milanese Sauce

2 cups ($\frac{1}{2}$ lb) sliced mushrooms
$\frac{1}{2}$ lb cooked ham, cut in julienne strips
2 tablespoons butter
$2\frac{1}{2}$ cups tomato sauce
$\frac{1}{2}$ cup freshly grated Parmesan cheese (to serve)

This sauce is excellent with macaroni, fusilli or other twisted pasta. If serving pasta as an accompaniment instead of as an entrée, use only $\frac{1}{4}$ lb each of mushrooms and ham for every $2\frac{1}{2}$ cups tomato sauce.

Method
Sauté mushrooms in the butter for 2–3 minutes until tender, then add the tomato sauce. Simmer 5 minutes and add the ham. Stir into the cooked pasta and toss over heat. Serve with freshly grated Parmesan cheese.

Napolitana Sauce

$1\frac{1}{2}$ lb Italian plum tomatoes, peeled, halved and seeded, or 3 cups canned plum tomatoes
1 medium onion, finely sliced
6 tablespoons butter or olive oil
clove of garlic, crushed
1 teaspoon tomato paste
1 tablespoon chopped basil
pinch of sugar
salt
black pepper, freshly ground
$\frac{1}{2}$ cup freshly grated Parmesan cheese (to serve)

This tomato sauce is not reduced as much as that in tomato sauce 2 and should be rougher in texture. It is very good with macaroni, spaghetti or noodles.

Method
In a skillet or shallow saucepan melt the butter or olive oil and sauté the onion until golden. Add the tomatoes with the garlic, tomato paste, basil, sugar and salt and pepper to taste and cook over medium heat for 15 minutes or until the tomatoes are pulpy but still have texture. Stir often to prevent them from sticking.

Taste for seasoning and toss with the cooked pasta, or spoon the sauce over the top. Serve freshly grated Parmesan cheese separately.

Tomato Sauce 1

1 can (2 lb) Italian plum tomatoes
1 tablespoon tomato paste
2 tablespoons butter
2 tablespoons flour
2 cups stock
salt and pepper
clove of garlic, crushed
bay leaf

Makes about 5 cups.

Method
Melt the butter in a saucepan, stir in the flour and cook until straw-colored. Blend in the tomato paste and stock and stir until the mixture boils. Add the tomatoes, crushing well with back of a wooden spoon. Stir in the salt, pepper, bay leaf and garlic. Cover pan and simmer 20–30 minutes or until fairly thick.

Work the mixture through a strainer into a bowl, taste for seasoning, then use as required.

Note: another version of tomato sauce was given in Volume 4.

Tomato Sauce 2

2 lb Italian plum tomatoes, or 4 cups canned plum tomatoes
$\frac{1}{4}$ cup butter or oil
1 onion, sliced
2 cloves of garlic, chopped
1 teaspoon mixed herbs (thyme, basil, oregano)
1 cup stock or water
salt and pepper
2–4 teaspoons tomato paste
2 tablespoons butter

This sauce ('sugo') is almost a purée, made without any additional thickening, and reduced to such a degree that it is red-brown in color and on the point of 'breaking' (curdling). This reduction gives the sauce its characteristic flavor – pungent and piquant – that blends well with spaghetti.

Make a double quantity when tomatoes are plentiful as it freezes well, or can be kept up to a week in the refrigerator. Makes about 3 cups.

Method
Wipe the tomatoes, halve them and squeeze out the seeds; slice them.

In a saucepan, melt the $\frac{1}{4}$ cup butter or oil, add the onion, garlic, tomatoes, herbs, stock or water and plenty of seasoning. Cover and cook 15–20 minutes or until thick and pulpy. Rub through a strainer, return the purée to the rinsed pan and add a little tomato paste to strengthen the flavor – the amount needed depends on the ripeness of the tomatoes. Add 2 tablespoons butter and simmer until thick, stirring often.

Toss tomato sauce with cooked spaghetti and serve with freshly grated Parmesan cheese.

Eggplant Salpicon

1 medium eggplant
2 green or red bell peppers
1 lb Italian plum tomatoes, peeled, seeded and sliced, or 2 cups canned plum tomatoes
6 tablespoons olive oil
2 medium onions, finely sliced
clove of garlic, crushed
5–6 anchovy fillets, chopped
$\frac{1}{2}$ teaspoon oregano, or basil
salt
black pepper, freshly ground
1 cup white wine

Salpicon is the name given to a mixture of ingredients that have been cut in shreds or fine strips. It may be served as a garnish, used as a stuffing for pastry cases and other dishes, or made into croquettes. Often the mixture is bound with a rich white or brown sauce.

This sauce is good with noodles or spaghetti.

Method
Wipe the eggplant and cut it in thin strips. Sprinkle with salt and leave 30 minutes to draw out the juice (dégorger). Rinse under cold water and dry on paper towels. Core and seed the peppers and cut them into thin strips; blanch in boiling water for 1 minute. Drain.

Sauté the eggplant strips in oil until brown, take out and add the onion and garlic, with a little extra oil if necessary. Sauté until soft, add the peppers, tomatoes, anchovies, oregano or basil and salt and pepper. Put back the eggplant and simmer the mixture gently for 10 minutes or until the eggplant is pulpy. Add the wine and simmer 5–6 minutes longer.

Serve this rich salpicon spooned over the top of the cooked pasta, or separately.

Sauce Conti

1 cup ($\frac{1}{4}$ lb) finely chopped mushrooms
$\frac{1}{4}$ cup chopped anchovy fillets
2 tablespoons butter
$\frac{1}{4}$ cup red wine vinegar
$\frac{1}{4}$ cup Marsala
2 cups chicken stock
3 egg yolks, beaten to mix
2 tablespoons capers
2 tablespoons Dijon-style mustard
pinch of cayenne

This sauce is good with spaghetti or linguine.

Method
In a saucepan sauté the mushrooms and anchovies in the butter until soft. Add the vinegar, Marsala and stock and simmer 20 minutes or until the sauce is reduced by one-third.

Gradually add a little of the hot sauce to the beaten egg yolks and stir the mixture into the remaining sauce, off the heat. Heat gently, stirring, until the sauce thickens slightly, but do not boil. Take from heat, add capers, mustard and cayenne, taste for seasoning and toss sauce with the cooked pasta.

Pesto Sauce

$\frac{1}{2}$ cup chopped fresh basil
4 fresh spinach leaves, chopped
2 tablespoons chopped parsley
6 tablespoons pine nuts
3 cloves of garlic, crushed
$\frac{1}{4}$ cup grated Parmesan cheese
$\frac{1}{4}$ cup grated Romano cheese
6 tablespoons olive oil
salt and pepper
$\frac{1}{2}$ cup extra grated Parmesan cheese (to serve)

Pesto is considered by many connoisseurs to be the finest of all pasta sauces. A spoonful of pesto is sometimes added to minestrone. The sauce can also be served with fish, and is very good with spaghetti or linguine.

Method
In a mortar and pestle pound the basil, spinach, parsley, pine nuts, garlic and both cheeses until the mixture is soft and smooth. Gradually beat in the oil, drop by drop, still pounding to make a smooth sauce. Season to taste and toss with hot pasta at the table; serve additional grated Parmesan cheese separately.

White Clam Sauce

24 cherrystone clams
1 onion, finely chopped
$\frac{1}{3}$ cup olive oil
2 cloves of garlic, crushed
$\frac{1}{4}$ cup chopped parsley
$\frac{1}{4}$ teaspoon crushed red pepper
pinch of basil
salt and pepper

This sauce is good with spaghetti or linguine.

Method
Wash the clams, discarding any with broken shells, and put them in a large kettle. Cover and cook over high heat, stirring once, until the shells open. Discard any that do not open and remove the clams from their shells.

In a saucepan sauté the onion in the oil until soft. Add the garlic and cook for 1 minute. Add the clams and the liquid from cooking, strained through cheesecloth, with the parsley, red pepper, basil and salt and pepper to taste. Heat thoroughly and toss at once with the cooked pasta.

Red Clam Sauce

24 cherrystone clams
2 onions, finely chopped
$\frac{1}{3}$ cup olive oil
$1\frac{1}{2}$ lb Italian plum tomatoes, peeled, seeded and chopped, or 3 cups canned plum tomatoes
3 cloves of garlic, crushed
1 teaspoon oregano
salt and pepper

This sauce is good with spaghetti or linguine.

Method
Wash the clams, discarding any with broken shells, and put into a large kettle. Cover and cook over high heat, stirring once, until the shells open. Discard any that do not open and remove the clams from the shells, reserving a few in their shells for decoration.

In a saucepan sauté the onions in the oil until golden. Add the tomatoes, garlic, oregano and salt and pepper to taste and simmer, uncovered and stirring occasionally, for 15 minutes or until the mixture is thick.

Strain the liquid from the cooked clams through cheesecloth and add to the tomato mixture with the clams. Heat thoroughly and mix half the sauce with the cooked pasta. Spoon the remaining sauce over the top, add the reserved clams in their shells and serve.

One of the finest pasta sauces, pesto sauce is excellent with spaghetti or linguine

Ruote (wheels) and fusilli (corkscrews) – shown here dried and cooked – are two of the many kinds of pasta shapes available. The cooked ruote and fusilli are served in tomato sauce 2 (recipe is on page 95)

KINDS OF PASTA

Twisted and twirled, flat or hollow, round or in shells, pasta shapes add a touch of fantasy to plain pasta. Particularly with small varieties of pasta added to soups, the Italian imagination runs riot with wheels, letters of the alphabet, twists or curls, and grains shaped like apple and melon seeds.

The long varieties (they are sometimes cut in short lengths too) – spaghetti, linguine, etc. – are generally served with a sauce and accompanied by freshly grated Parmesan cheese. The twisted pasta like fusilli and hollow types like macaroni absorb more sauce and thus make richer dishes than the flat or circular shapes.

The largest kinds of pasta are for stuffing – grooved rigatoni or shell-shaped conchiglie make a pleasant change from the familiar canneloni although they taste the same.

There are more than 40 different shapes of pasta with their own names and in Italy you will come across dozens of anonymous ones, created by the ingenuity of the local grocery store. The shapes on the next page are the most widely known.

KINDS OF PASTA *continued*

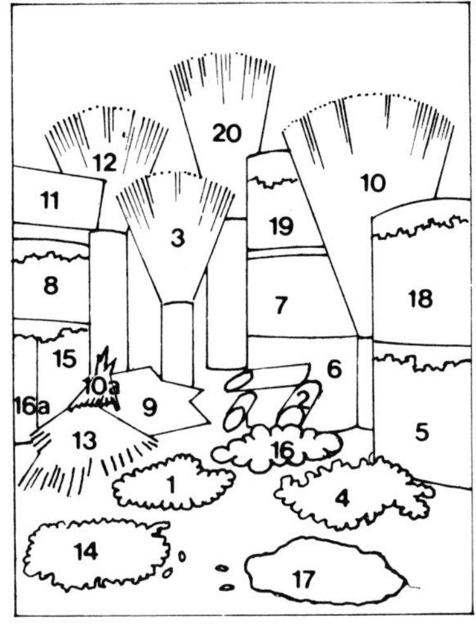

1 Anelli (rings): used in soups. They also come in little rings (anellini) and grooved little rings (anellini rigati).

2 Canneloni: large hollow pasta, usually stuffed with chicken or veal, or ricotta cheese mixed with prosciutto, garlic, parsley and other typically Italian flavors. They can also be flat squares of pasta rolled around a filling.

3 Capelline (little hairs): very, very fine pasta; round like spaghetti, they come in little folded nests like noodles.

4 Coloroni (vegetable macaroni): ordinary macaroni to which the manufacturer has added vegetable coloring: spinach for the green color, tomato for the red.

5 Conchiglie (sea shells): made plain or grooved, they also come in two other sizes: **conchigliette** (tiny shells) and **conchigliette piccole** (very tiny shells). The piccole are used in soups.

6 Egg noodles: theoretically always made with eggs, thus producing a different, richer flavor than the usual pasta. Noodles come in a variety of widths; they can be ruffled or rippled on one side, and they are available in long straight lengths, in little skeins or bundles and in twists or curls.

7 Elbow macaroni: one of the most familiar of the pasta, is a semicircular macaroni, hollow inside and ranging in size from small to quite large. Interestingly enough, even the Italian manufacturers use the English word 'elbow' on the package.

8 Farfalle (butterflies): bow-shaped egg pasta, made in many sizes (the Italians use a plain pasta, mainly made of flour and water).

9 Fettucine verde: one of the best known of the Italian noodles, green in color and sold in straight lengths or loosely bent and curled. Plain fettucine can also be bought in the natural color, creamy white.

10 Fusilli: long rods of spaghetti twisted like a corkscrew.

10a There is a second variety known as 'twists with a hole'. These **fusilli bucati** are made of thin macaroni, hence the hole in the middle.

11 Lasagne: wide to very wide strips of flat pasta, frequently made with one or both sides rippled. They come in two colors, the natural creamy white color or the green, made with a little spinach. Recipes will be given in Volume 8.

12 Linguine: resemble flattened spaghetti, ranging in width from fine to broad. They, too, appear in markets as creamy white or green.

Macaroni: hollow tubes of pasta sold in lengths or in short curved pieces.

Manicotti: large tubes of pasta.

13 Mezze zite: large, tubular macaroni, frequently as long as spaghetti and broken into pieces before cooking.

14 Orzo means barley, but the tiny pasta of this name look more like ordinary grains of rice. Orzo can be used in soup but also make an excellent substitute for rice or potatoes.

15 Rigatoni: large, grooved pasta tubes. Except for manicotti, rigatoni are the largest of the well-known tube pastas.

16 Ruote (wheels) are so realistic that they come with hub, spokes and grooved rim. They also come in small wheels **(rotelle)** and small accordions **(ruotine)**. Then come the smallest wheels of all **(rotelline)**. **Ruote,** in all sizes, are mainly used in soups.

17 Semi di melone are little bits of pasta that look like the seeds of a melon; there are even smaller ones called **semi di mela** (apple seeds). Both are used in soups.

Spaghetti: long rods in varying thicknesses; the very thin type is vermicelli.

Tagliatelle: ribbon pasta similar to noodles, varying in width. It comes plain, or flavored with spinach or tomato.

18 Tortiglioni: another variety of closely twisted pasta, this time cut in short lengths.

19 Twistetti: hollow or pierced pasta of the macaroni type. This member of the family is twisted and curly.

20 Vermicelli (little 'worms'): very thin, rod-like spaghetti. Occasionally it can be found in folded form, not unlike the folded skeins of noodles seen in some markets.

Cooking with Apples and Pears

Apples and pears used to be almost the only fruits that could be stored until the middle of winter and so were available for more than half the year. As a result, innumerable homey, traditional recipes have been developed to use them. These fruits can be poached, baked, fried and occasionally even broiled; served for dessert and as accompaniments for savory dishes. They are the basis of all kinds of jams, butters, chutneys and jellies; they are added to cakes and chopped for stuffings.

Both apples and pears fall into two general categories – those good for cooking that have a tart, distinctive flavor, and the sweeter dessert varieties. Sometimes these categories overlap when dessert fruit has enough acidity to be good for cooking.

Fruit for poaching should have a firm flesh and can be slightly less ripe than for eating out of hand. Fruit for baking or making a purée should have a softer flesh that will become light and fluffy when cooked.

Both apples and pears turn brown quickly after they are pared. If the surface is rubbed with a cut lemon or the fruit is soaked in water and lemon juice, browning will be retarded, but the fruit should always be cooked or eaten as soon as possible after paring.

Points to remember

To make a syrup for whole or quartered apples and pears: dissolve 3–4 tablespoons sugar in 1 cup water for every lb of fruit. Add a strip of lemon peel (or for **vanilla syrup** a piece of vanilla bean) for flavor and boil the syrup for 2 minutes.

To poach fruit in syrup
Firm dessert apples like Golden Delicious or pears like Bosc, Anjou or Bartlett are best for poaching. Pare and core the fruit and leave whole or cut in halves or quarters according to the recipe. Immerse in the syrup with the rounded part of the fruit at the bottom of the pan. Let the syrup boil up and over the fruit, then reduce the heat, cover the pan, and let cook very gently for 15–20 minutes or until the fruit is transparent. To prevent discoloration after cooking, be sure the fruit is completely cooked. Let cool in the syrup and remove the lemon rind or vanilla bean.

To make apple sauce
Pare, quarter and core tart apples. Slice, measure and place them in a saucepan, add 2 tablespoons sugar, 2 tablespoons water and the grated rind of 1 lemon per 2 cups sliced apples. Cover the apples with buttered brown paper, press it down on top, add the lid and cook very gently to a pulp, stirring occasionally. Crush well with a potato masher or beat well with a wooden spoon. Taste the sauce and add more sugar if needed.

For some recipes this mixture may be worked through a sieve or puréed in a blender.

To make a 'marmelade' purée
Wash tart apples, wipe, quarter and core them. Thickly butter a heavy flameproof casserole and put the apples into the pan. Add a strip of lemon rind, cover with a piece of buttered brown paper and a lid and cook gently until soft, stirring occasionally. Remove the lemon rind and purée in a blender or work through a sieve.

Rinse out the pot, return the purée to it and add 3–4 tablespoons sugar per cup of purée, or to taste. Cook rapidly on top of the stove, stirring constantly, or bake in a moderately hot oven (375°F) until the mixture is stiff but still falls easily from a spoon. When cold, this marmelade sets firmly like apple butter. Use to fill pies, flans and cakes.

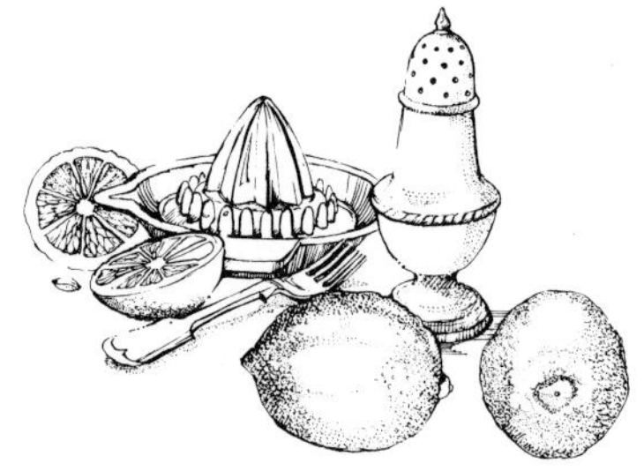

Swedish Apple Charlotte
with Apricot Jam Sauce

6 medium tart apples
$\frac{1}{4}$ cup sugar
$\frac{1}{2}$ cup butter
1 cup fresh white breadcrumbs
1 cup apricot jam sauce, or $\frac{1}{2}$ cup heavy cream, stiffly whipped (to serve)

Charlotte mold, or deep soufflé dish (1 quart capacity)

Method
Cook the apples to a marmelade purée and add the sugar.

In a frying pan melt the butter and fry breadcrumbs until golden brown. Fill the buttered charlotte mold or soufflé dish with alternate layers of fried crumbs and apple purée, beginning and ending with crumbs. Bake in a moderately hot oven (375°F) for about 30 minutes or until the mixture is firm and the top is brown.

Turn the charlotte out onto a platter and serve the apricot jam sauce or whipped cream separately.

Apricot Jam Sauce

For 1 cup: heat 6 tablespoons apricot jam with $\frac{3}{4}$ cup water and grated rind and juice of 1 lemon, stirring until the jam has dissolved. Bring to a boil, take from heat and stir in 1 teaspoon arrowroot (mixed to a paste with 1 tablespoon cold water). Heat, stirring, until the sauce thickens. Strain before serving.

Baked Apples

Choose large and firm tart apples without blemishes and allow 1 per person. Wipe and core them with the end of a vegetable peeler – this way you can scoop out the core without making a hole all the way through the apple. Slit the skin horizontally around the middle of each apple.

Fill each cavity with a mixture of white or brown sugar and golden raisins and place the apples in an ovenproof dish. Add 2–3 tablespoons water and top each apple with 1 tablespoon butter. Bake the apples in a moderately hot oven (375°F) for about 40 minutes or until tender – the cooking time will vary with the variety of apple. Baste once or twice with the juices in the pan.

Serve warm or cool with whipped cream, sour cream, or ice cream.

Chocolate Baked Apples

Prepare the apples as above but fill each cavity with 1 square (1 oz) semisweet chocolate, divided in half. Spoon 1 tablespoon molasses over each apple, add 2–3 tablespoons water and bake as before.

Almond Baked Apples

Prepare the apples as above, then mash 5 tablespoons almond paste with 1–2 tablespoons rum and work in 2 tablespoons currants. Fill each cavity with a little butter, some of the almond paste mixture and top each one with a pat of butter. Bake as before.

Baked apples are good served with whipped cream, sour cream or ice cream

Apple Brown Betty

6 tart apples
4–5 thin slices of dry white bread
2 tablespoons butter, softened
4–5 tablespoons golden syrup or honey
1 cup heavy cream (for serving) – optional

Deep ovenproof dish ($1\frac{1}{2}$–2 quart capacity)

Method
Cut crusts from the bread, thickly butter each slice and cut into four. Pare, core and thinly slice the apples.

Place a layer of bread at the bottom of the dish, cover with about half the apple slices and 1 tablespoon golden syrup or honey. Cover with a second layer of bread and fill with the remaining apple slices and another tablespoon of golden syrup or honey.

Arrange the rest of the bread, overlapping, to cover the surface of the apples and spread with remaining golden syrup or honey. Bake in a moderately hot oven (375°F) for 40–50 minutes or until brown and crisp. Serve with heavy cream.

Golden syrup is a sweet syrup popular in England and made as a by-product when refining sugar. The flavor is a cross between honey and molasses. Golden syrup is now available in many supermarkets.

Eve's Pudding

5 large tart apples
$\frac{1}{4}$ cup sugar
juice of $\frac{1}{2}$ lemon
2 tablespoons water

For topping
$1\frac{1}{4}$ cups self-rising flour
pinch of salt
6 tablespoons butter
grated rind of $\frac{1}{2}$ lemon
6 tablespoons sugar
1 large egg
2–3 tablespoons milk

Ovenproof dish, or soufflé dish ($1\frac{1}{2}$ quart capacity)

Method
Pare and core the apples, cut in thick slices and put in a pan with the $\frac{1}{4}$ cup of sugar, lemon juice and water. Cover and cook until the apples are tender. Spread in the dish.

To make the topping: sift the flour with the salt. Cream the butter with the lemon rind in a bowl, add the sugar and beat until light and soft. Beat in the egg and, with a metal spoon, fold in the flour. Stir in enough milk so that the mixture drops easily from a spoon and spread it over the apples.

Bake the pudding in a moderately hot oven (375°F) for 35–40 minutes or until risen and brown. Serve hot.

Apple Tart Tatin

5 medium Golden Delicious apples
$\frac{1}{4}$ cup butter
$\frac{1}{2}$ cup sugar
1 cup quantity of rough puff pastry (see Volume 2)
1 cup heavy cream, stiffly whipped (for serving)

8 inch square cake pan, or 9 inch pie pan

This upside-down pie with its caramel topping is a specialty of Maxim's in Paris.

Method
Set oven at hot (425°F). Generously butter the pan and sprinkle over half the sugar. Pare, core and thinly slice the apples and arrange, overlapping, in the pan. Sprinkle each layer with remaining sugar and dot with butter.

Roll out the pastry dough to cover the pan, lift it on top of the apples and tuck a fold of dough inside around the edge of the pan to allow for shrinkage. Trim the dough and make a hole for steam to escape in the center. Chill 30 minutes.

Bake the tart in heated oven for 10 minutes, turn down the heat to 375°F and bake 45–50 minutes longer or until the pastry is brown and the apples are tender when tested with a skewer through the center hole.

Lift a corner of the pastry and sniff to see if the sugar at the bottom of the pan has caramelized – the odor is unmistakable. If not, place pan on top of stove over very low heat until sugar caramelizes.

Cool the tart to lukewarm, then turn it out, bottom side up, onto a platter – the top should be golden with caramel. Serve with whipped cream.

Apple Snow

6 tart apples
2 egg whites
$\frac{1}{2}$ cup sugar
1 tablespoon rum or vanilla (to taste)
orange and/or lemon juice (to taste)

Method
Set oven at hot (400°F).

Wash the apples and pat them dry with paper towels. Stand them, unpared and whole, in a roasting pan with about 1 inch of water in the bottom. Bake in heated oven for 30–40 minutes or until the apples are tender but still hold their shape. Slice the apples in half, remove seeds and cores and work the apples through a food mill. If you wish, purée the apples in a blender but remove the skins before blending. Chill the apple purée.

Beat the egg whites until they hold a stiff peak and gradually beat in the sugar a few tablespoons at a time, to form a stiff, shiny meringue. With a large metal spoon, fold meringue into the chilled apple purée, with rum or vanilla and a little orange and/or lemon juice for flavor.

When the meringue is combined, beat hard until the mixture is foamy. Spoon into a glass bowl or individual serving dishes and chill 3–4 hours before serving.

Apples Bristol

4 large Golden Delicious apples
3 oranges
$\frac{1}{2}$ cup sugar
$1\frac{1}{2}$ cups water
strip of lemon rind, or $\frac{1}{2}$ teaspoon vanilla

For caramel
6 tablespoons sugar
$\frac{1}{2}$ cup water

Method

Make a syrup by dissolving the $\frac{1}{2}$ cup sugar in $1\frac{1}{2}$ cups water. Bring to a boil and flavor with lemon rind or vanilla. Pare, core and quarter the apples, immerse them in syrup, cover and simmer 15 minutes or until just tender. Take from heat but leave the pan covered until cold – the apples should look almost transparent.

With a vegetable peeler, thinly peel the rind from half an orange and cut in fine strips. Blanch in boiling water for 5 minutes or until tender; drain and rinse well with cold water. Cut the remaining rind and skin from the oranges and slice the orange flesh into rounds.

Drain the apples and place in a serving bowl, arrange the orange slices on top and add enough syrup from the apples to cover. Chill.

To make the caramel: dissolve the sugar in the water, bring to a boil and cook to a rich brown. Pour at once into an oiled pan and cool until set.

Crush the caramel into fairly small pieces in a mortar and pestle or with a rolling pin and scatter with orange strips over the oranges and the apples just before serving.

Watchpoint: the caramel will dissolve if it is added more than 1 hour before serving.

Apple Amber (Apple Meringue)

6 tart apples
$\frac{1}{3}$ cup sugar
grated rind and juice of 1 lemon
3 tablespoons butter
3 egg yolks

For meringue Suisse
3 egg whites
small pinch of salt
$\frac{3}{4}$ cup sugar
sugar (for sprinkling)

Shallow ovenproof dish, or soufflé dish ($1\frac{1}{2}$ quart capacity)

Method

Make the apple sauce with the apples (see page 104), add the sugar and flavor with lemon rind and juice.

While the purée is hot, beat in the butter, a small piece at a time, followed by the egg yolks. Pour the mixture into the dish.

Beat the egg whites in a bowl with the salt until they hold a stiff peak. Beat in 1 tablespoon of the measured sugar; continue beating for 1 minute. Fold in the remaining sugar with a metal spoon and pile on top of the apple mixture. Sprinkle generously with sugar. Bake in a moderately low oven (325°F) for 30 minutes or until the top is crisp and golden brown.

Chantilly Cream

For 1 cup: whip $\frac{1}{2}$ cup heavy cream until it starts to thicken; add 2 teaspoons sugar and pinch of vanilla; continue whipping until cream holds a shape.

Apples and Pears with Almond Meringue

6 tart apples
4 firm ripe pears
$\frac{1}{4}$ cup sugar (or to taste)
1 tablespoon butter
grated rind and juice of 1 lemon
$1\frac{1}{2}$ cups vanilla-flavored sugar syrup (see page 104)
confectioners' sugar (for sprinkling)

For almond meringue cuite
2 egg whites
1 cup confectioners' sugar
small pinch of salt
1 teaspoon vanilla
$\frac{1}{2}$ cup slivered almonds

Ovenproof dish, or soufflé dish ($1\frac{1}{2}$ quart capacity)

Method

Make a marmelade with the apples (see page 104), add sugar and butter, and flavor with lemon rind and juice. Pare and quarter the pears, scooping out the cores with a teaspoon; poach the pears in syrup until tender and let cool. Butter the dish.

To make the almond meringue: sift the confectioners' sugar through a fine sieve onto a sheet of wax paper; if beating by hand, have a pan half-full of gently simmering water ready.

Beat the egg whites and salt with a rotary or electric beater until foaming. Beat in the confectioners' sugar a teaspoon at a time and, when all of it is added, beat in the vanilla. If beating by hand, set the bowl over hot water and continue beating until the mixture holds its shape. No heat is necessary if using an electric beater. When ready, the mixture will form a stiff, tall peak when a little is lifted on the beater. With a metal spoon, carefully fold in the slivered almonds.

Spread the apple purée in the prepared dish, arrange the drained pears on top and cover with meringue. Sprinkle generously with confectioners' sugar and bake in a moderate oven (350°F) for 20 minutes or until brown.

Apple Crisp

6 tart apples
$\frac{1}{2}$ cup sugar
2 teaspoons lemon juice
$\frac{1}{2}$ teaspoon ground cinnamon
$\frac{1}{4}$ teaspoon ground cloves
1 cup Chantilly cream (see box)

For topping
$\frac{3}{4}$ cup flour
pinch of salt
6 tablespoons butter
$\frac{1}{2}$ cup sugar
$\frac{1}{4}$ cup chopped hazelnuts or almonds

Baking dish ($2\frac{1}{2}$–3 quart capacity)

Method

Set oven at moderate (350°F) and butter the baking dish.

Pare and core the apples and cut them into thin slices in a bowl. Mix the apples with the sugar, lemon juice, cinnamon and cloves and spoon into the prepared dish.

In a bowl sift the flour and salt together. Work in the butter with the fingertips until the mixture resembles breadcrumbs. Stir in the sugar and chopped nuts and sprinkle the mixture over the apples. Bake in heated oven for 45 minutes or until the apples are tender and the topping is golden brown. Serve warm with Chantilly cream.

Pears poached gently in red wine sauce make an unusual dessert

Pears in Red Wine

5–6 firm, ripe pears
10 tablespoons sugar
$\frac{3}{4}$ cup water
$\frac{3}{4}$ cup red wine
strip of lemon rind
1 inch piece of cinnamon stick
1 teaspoon arrowroot, mixed to a paste with 1 tablespoon water
$\frac{1}{4}$ cup slivered almonds, browned (optional)
$\frac{1}{2}$ cup heavy cream, stiffly whipped (for serving) – optional

Method

To make the syrup: in a deep pan dissolve the sugar in the water and wine, add lemon rind and cinnamon stick, bring to a boil and cook 1 minute.

Keep the stems on the pears, pare and remove the 'eye' from the bases. Place the pears in the prepared syrup so they are completely covered, cover the pan and poach the pears until tender. Even when the pears are ripe this must take 20–30 minutes to prevent discoloring around the cores.

Drain the pears and arrange in a serving bowl. Strain the syrup – it should have reduced to $1\frac{1}{4}$ cups during cooking; if not, continue boiling it.

Stir the arrowroot paste liaison into the hot syrup and heat until the sauce thickens. Take it at once from the heat, cool slightly and spoon over the pears. Chill thoroughly and sprinkle browned almonds over the dish. If you like, serve whipped cream separately.

Pears in Ginger

4 pears
$\frac{3}{4}$ cup sugar
$\frac{3}{4}$ cup water
few pieces of candied ginger, chopped
$\frac{1}{2}$ cup heavy cream, stiffly whipped (to serve)

Method

Dissolve the sugar in the water, add the pieces of ginger, and bring the syrup to a boil.

Pare and halve the pears, scoop out the cores with a teaspoon and immerse at once in sugar syrup, rounded side down. Cover and simmer gently for 15–20 minutes or until the pears are tender. Let cool in the syrup.

Serve with whipped cream.

Pears in Orange Cream

4–6 firm, ripe pears
$\frac{1}{4}$ cup sugar
$1\frac{1}{2}$ cups water

For custard
$\frac{3}{4}$ cup milk
2 egg yolks
1 teaspoon arrowroot
1–2 teaspoons sugar

For orange cream
rind and juice of 1 large orange
5 cubes of sugar
$\frac{3}{4}$ cup heavy cream, whipped until it holds a soft shape

Method

To make the syrup: dissolve the sugar in the water and bring the syrup to a boil.

Pare and halve the pears, scoop out the cores with a teaspoon and immerse at once in the sugar syrup, rounded side down. Cover and simmer gently for 15–20 minutes or until the pears are tender. Let cool in the syrup.

With a vegetable peeler, thinly peel the rind from half the orange and cut it into fine strips. Blanch for 5 minutes in boiling water or until tender, drain and rinse well.

To make the custard: scald the milk in a pan. Beat the egg yolks with the arrowroot and sugar until thick and light. Gradually stir in the milk and return the custard to the pan. Heat, stirring, until it thickens enough to coat the back of a wooden spoon. Do not boil. Strain the custard, cover with plastic wrap to prevent a skin from forming and cool.

To make the orange cream: rub the sugar cubes over the rind of the remaining half of orange to remove the zest (oil) – the sugar should be saturated with oil. Squeeze the orange and pour 5 tablespoons juice over the sugar cubes in a bowl and stir until the sugar is dissolved. Stir this orange syrup with the cooled custard into the whipped cream.

Drain the pears, arrange in a deep serving dish and coat with the orange cream. Sprinkle the orange strips over the top.

Browned Almonds

Bake blanched almonds in a moderately hot oven (375°F) for 8–10 minutes or until browned.

Sauté of duck, with espagnole sauce spooned over, is garnished with stuffed mushrooms (recipe is on page 115)

Duck is one of the luxurious entrées you can make for this menu or there is a choice of a rack of lamb, roasted with a crisp breadcrumb and herb crust and served with a Béarnaise sauce. For a special dessert, try the oranges stuffed with candied fruits and topped with meringue.

With either the duck or the lamb, a full-bodied claret would be ideal. Among the very best are the rousing reds from Pomerol, that famous wine district on the right bank of the Dordogne in Bordeaux. A suitable alternative from vineyards closer to home would be a top quality California Cabernet Sauvignon.

SAUTE DUCK IN A RICH WINE SAUCE

Shrimps Ritz

Sauté of Duck with Mushrooms
Green Peas Boiled New Potatoes

or

Roast Lamb Gratiné
Spinach Boiled New Potatoes

Oranges en Surprise

Red wine – Pomerol (Bordeaux)
or Cabernet Sauvignon (California)

TIMETABLE

Day before
Cook and peel the shrimps and refrigerate. Make tomato sauce and mayonnaise for shrimps, cover and keep in cool place.
Make Espagnole sauce for the duck.

Morning
Complete sauce Ritz for the shrimps; wash the lettuce and keep in a plastic bag in refrigerator.
Cut duck in pieces and refrigerate; make the mushroom garnish and keep covered.
Prepare lamb for roasting and keep in refrigerator; make breadcrumb coating.
Prepare all vegetables.
Scoop out the oranges and macerate candied fruits. Keep the orange flesh and shells covered.

Assemble ingredients for final cooking from 6:50 for dinner around 8 p.m.

You will find that **cooking times** given in the individual recipes for these dishes have sometimes been adapted in the timetable to help you when cooking and serving this menu as a party meal.

Order of Work

6:50
Set oven at hot (400°F).
Make meringue cuite, pipe on top of oranges, brown in oven and chill.

7:00
Start browning duck.

7:15
Flame the duck, cover it and leave to simmer gently.
Start roasting the lamb. Make Béarnaise sauce; keep warm.

7:30
Boil potatoes; cook peas *or spinach.*

7:35
Add the breadcrumb topping to the lamb.
Finish shrimps Ritz, cover and chill.

7:45
Drain the vegetables and reserve.
Arrange the duck on a platter and keep warm; finish sauce. Cook the mushroom garnish and add to the platter.

7:55
Transfer the lamb to a platter and keep warm; reduce gravy and add to Béarnaise sauce.
Reheat vegetables in butter, put in serving dishes and keep warm.

8:00
Serve shrimps Ritz.

Appetizer

Shrimps Ritz

1 lb cooked, peeled shrimps
juice of ½ lemon
black pepper, freshly ground
few lettuce leaves
paprika (for sprinkling)

For sauce Ritz
¼ cup tomato sauce
1 cup mayonnaise
1 celery heart, chopped, or 1 cucumber, peeled, seeds removed and finely diced
½ large green bell pepper, cored, seeded and finely diced
1½ tablespoons prepared horseradish
clove of garlic, crushed
2–3 tablespoons heavy cream
few drops of Tabasco
salt

Method
Put the shrimps in a bowl and sprinkle with lemon juice and black pepper. Cover and let marinate about 30 minutes. If using cucumber, sprinkle with salt and let stand 15 minutes to draw out the juices (dégorger), then rinse with cold water, drain thoroughly and dry on paper towels.

To make sauce Ritz: mix the tomato sauce with the mayonnaise and stir in the celery or cucumber, green pepper, horseradish, garlic, cream, Tabasco and salt. Taste and add more of the seasonings, if necessary, to make the sauce spicy and quite piquant.

Drain the shrimps and arrange on lettuce leaves on individual plates. Coat the shrimps with 2–3 tablespoons sauce. Sprinkle with paprika and chill before serving. If you like, the lettuce can be shredded and put into individual glass bowls with the shrimps and sauce on top. Set the bowls on a bed of ice, if you like.

Mayonnaise

2 egg yolks
¼ teaspoon salt
pinch of pepper
pinch of dry mustard
¾ cup oil
2 tablespoons wine vinegar

Makes 1 cup.

Method
In a bowl, beat the egg yolks and seasonings with a small whisk or wooden spoon until thick. Add the oil, drop by drop; when 2 tablespoons have been added, the mixture will be very thick. Stir in 1 teaspoon vinegar.

The remaining oil can be added more quickly (1 tablespoon at a time, beaten thoroughly between each addition until smooth, or in a thin steady stream if using an electric blender). When all the oil has been used, add remaining vinegar with more seasoning to taste.

To thin and lighten mayonnaise, add a little hot water. For a coating consistency, thin with a little cream or milk.
Watchpoint: mayonnaise curdles easily, so be sure to add the oil drop by drop at first; and continue adding it *very* slowly until very thick, after which you can speed up. If mayonnaise does curdle, start with a fresh yolk in another bowl and work well with seasonings. Then add the curdled mixture drop by drop. To lessen the chances of curdling, have all ingredients at room temperature before starting.

Serve shrimps Ritz in attractive glass bowls on a bed of ice

Using scissors or poultry shears, cut the duck into 6 neat pieces before sautéing them in butter until lightly browned

For garnish for the duck, fill each sautéed mushroom cap with stuffing mixture, doming it in the center

Lamb gratiné with its crisp breadcrumb topping is served carved into cutlets

Entrée

Sauté of Duck with Mushrooms

4–5 lb duck, including liver
$1\frac{1}{2}$ cups espagnole sauce (see Volume 2)
$\frac{1}{4}$ cup Madeira or sherry
$1\frac{1}{2}$ tablespoons butter
$\frac{1}{4}$ cup brandy
1 small onion, finely chopped
salt and pepper

For garnish
2 cups ($\frac{1}{2}$ lb) large mushrooms
1 shallot or scallion, finely chopped
3 tablespoons butter
2 tablespoons fresh white breadcrumbs
1 teaspoon mixed herbs (thyme, tarragon, oregano)
1 tablespoon grated Parmesan cheese

Method

Prepare the espagnole sauce. After straining the sauce, add the Madeira or sherry, continue simmering for 5–6 minutes, then set aside. Sauté the duck liver until lightly browned in $\frac{1}{2}$ tablespoon butter, cool, cut it in slices and add to the sauce.

Cut the duck into 6 neat pieces and sauté them slowly in the remaining butter for 15–20 minutes. When thoroughly browned and most of the outer fat has been extracted, pour off all but 1 tablespoon fat. Add the brandy, flame and after about 1 minute, stir in the onion and seasoning. Cover and cook over low heat for 20 minutes or until the duck pieces are tender.

To prepare the garnish: remove mushroom stems, chop them finely and add to the shallot or scallion. Melt 1 tablespoon butter in a saucepan, add the chopped mushroom mixture, cook $\frac{1}{2}$ minute until soft and add the breadcrumbs and herbs. Take from the pan and set aside. Add the remaining butter to the pan and sauté the mushroom caps very lightly until tender. Remove them and fill each one with the stuffing mixture, doming it in the center. Sprinkle with Parmesan cheese and brown them under the broiler or bake them in a hot oven (425°F) for 5–6 minutes.

Transfer the duck to a warm serving platter and keep hot. If necessary, reduce the liquid in the pan to 3–4 tablespoons and strain it into the espagnole sauce. Reheat the sauce carefully and spoon a little over the duck. Garnish the platter with mushrooms and serve the remaining sauce in a sauce boat. Serve the duck with green peas and small boiled new potatoes tossed in butter.

Alternative entrée

Roast Lamb Gratiné

$2\frac{1}{2}$–3 lb rack of lamb
2 cloves of garlic, peeled and cut in slivers
$\frac{1}{4}$ cup butter
black pepper, freshly ground
1 cup white wine
$\frac{1}{3}$ cup fresh white breadcrumbs
2 tablespoons melted butter
1 tablespoon chopped parsley
1 egg yolk

For Béarnaise sauce
3 tablespoons wine vinegar (or tarragon vinegar if no fresh tarragon is available)
3 shallots, chopped
2–3 sprigs of tarragon or $\frac{1}{2}$ teaspoon dried tarragon
2 egg yolks
salt and pepper
6 tablespoons unsalted butter, softened
1 tablespoon chopped parsley, or tarragon and parsley mixed

For this dish the Béarnaise sauce must be very strongly flavored with tarragon. A small (4–5 lb) leg of lamb may be used instead of the rack; allow 1–$1\frac{1}{2}$ hours total roasting time for the leg.

Method

Set oven at hot (400°F). Cut incisions with a small pointed knife in the bone side of the lamb and stick a sliver of garlic into each incision. Spread the meat generously with butter, grind over a little pepper and set the meat, bone side down, in a roasting pan. Pour over $\frac{1}{2}$ cup wine and roast in heated oven for 20–25 minutes; baste often.

To make Béarnaise sauce: in a small pan put the wine vinegar or tarragon vinegar, shallot and fresh or dried tarragon. Boil the mixture until reduced to 1 tablespoon and set the pan aside. Beat the egg yolks with a pinch of salt and 1 tablespoon butter in a bowl or the top of a double boiler. Strain in the vinegar mixture and set the bowl over a pan of boiling water or set the boiler top over the double boiler. Remove from heat and stir until the sauce begins to thicken. Add the remaining butter, piece by piece, stirring all the time – it should be warm, not hot. Season with pepper and keep warm in a water bath.

Watchpoint: do not let the sauce get too hot or it will curdle.

Mix the breadcrumbs, melted butter, parsley and egg yolk together. After the meat has roasted for 20–25 minutes, take it out of the oven and press the breadcrumb mixture on the fat side, smoothing it with a knife; baste the lamb carefully. Return the meat to the oven for about 15–20 minutes longer or until lightly browned and a meat thermometer inserted in the center registers 160°F for medium done meat. Transfer the meat to a heated platter and keep warm.

Deglaze the roasting pan with the remaining $\frac{1}{2}$ cup wine, cook until reduced to about 2 tablespoons, then strain and add to Béarnaise sauce with the chopped herbs.

Watchpoint: it is important that the concentrated gravy from the lamb be added to the Béarnaise sauce only just before serving.

Serve lamb with chopped spinach tossed with butter and a pinch of nutmeg, and boiled new potatoes tossed in butter. Serve sauce separately.

Oranges en Surprise

5–6 large navel oranges
2–3 tablespoons Grand Marnier, Curaçao, Triple Sec, or other orange liqueur
1 cup chopped mixed candied fruits (cherries, ginger, orange, lemon and citron peel)
2 egg white quantity meringue cuite (see box)
sugar (for sprinkling)

Pastry bag and a medium star tube

The oranges, with meringue cuite piped on top, can be prepared and browned 1–2 hours ahead and kept in the refrigerator.

Method
Set oven at hot (400°F). Pour the orange liqueur over the candied fruits, cover and leave to macerate.

Slice the tops off the oranges and, with a grapefruit knife, scoop out the flesh. Discard the core and as much of the membrane as possible. Mix the orange flesh with the candied fruits and pile back into the orange shells. Chill them.

Make the meringue cuite, fill into the pastry bag fitted with the star tube and pipe meringue on top of each orange. Place them in a roasting pan, filled with ice cubes, sprinkle generously with sugar and bake in heated oven for 5–10 minutes or until meringue is browned. Serve cool.

Watchpoint: the meringue must brown quickly because oranges have a marmalade taste if they start to cook.

Pile the candied fruits – that have been macerated in liqueur – with the orange flesh into the orange shells and chill well

Meringue Cuite

Sift 2 cups confectioners' sugar through a fine sieve onto a sheet of wax paper.

Beat 4 egg whites with a rotary or electric beater until frothy. Beat in the confectioners' sugar 1 teaspoon at a time and, when all of it is added, beat in 1 teaspoon vanilla. If beating by hand, have a pan half-full of gently simmering water ready; set the bowl over the hot water and continue beating until the mixture holds its shape. No heat is needed if using an electric beater.

To test, lift a little of the mixture on the beater; if ready it should form a stiff tall peak.

Fill the pastry bag fitted with a star tube with the meringue cuite and pipe it on top of the orange shells to cover the fruit completely

For an unusual dessert, oranges en surprise are filled with candied fruits

Stuffed trout is served with small buttered onions and peas (recipe is on page 126)

AROUND THE WORLD DISHES

Take a break from routine recipes and try some of the dishes you might taste away from home. Here on the following pages are a few suggestions from around the world.

Turkish Meatball Soup

1 lb ground raw lamb
1 tablespoon butter
1 onion, chopped
1 cup cooked rice
$\frac{1}{4}$ teaspoon cayenne
salt and pepper
$\frac{1}{4}$ cup chopped parsley
4 cups beef stock
1 cup white wine
juice of 1 lemon
2 egg yolks, beaten to mix

Method

In a skillet melt the butter and fry the onion until soft. In a bowl combine the onion, lamb, rice, cayenne and salt and pepper to taste and work together with the hands. Wet the palms of the hands and shape into walnut-size balls. Roll the balls in parsley.

Boil the stock and wine in a pan until reduced to 4 cups.

Arrange the balls in a saucepan and pour over the stock and wine mixture. Simmer gently for 30 minutes. Gradually beat the lemon juice into the egg yolks, stir in a little hot soup and add this mixture to the remaining soup, off the heat. Spoon into bowls and serve, sprinkled with remaining parsley.

Greek Stewed Lamb with Chicory and Avgolemono Sauce

$2\frac{1}{2}$–3 lb lamb shanks or lamb shoulder chops
large head of chicory or escarole
3 tablespoons olive oil
2 onions, chopped
2–$2\frac{1}{2}$ cups water
salt and pepper

For avgolemono sauce
2 eggs
juice of 1 lemon

Method

In a flameproof casserole heat the oil and brown the lamb on all sides, a few pieces at a time. Take out, add the onion and cook over medium heat until browned. Replace the lamb, add the water and seasoning and simmer on top of the stove or in a moderately low oven (325°F) for 1–$1\frac{1}{2}$ hours or until the lamb is almost tender. Add more water if the pan gets dry.

Separate the chicory or escarole leaves into 3 inch lengths, wash well, blanch in boiling water for 1 minute and drain. Add chicory or escarole to lamb, cover and simmer 15 minutes longer or until both are tender.

To make avgolemono sauce: beat the eggs in a bowl until fluffy and light-colored. Gradually add the lemon juice, beating constantly. Stir in about $\frac{1}{2}$ cup hot cooking liquid from the lamb and pour this mixture back into the pot. Shake pot so cooking liquid and egg mixture combine; let stand in a warm place for 5 minutes so sauce thickens.

Watchpoint: do not let boil or it will curdle.

Taste for seasoning; serve the stew with boiled rice.

Fritto Misto with Alabama Sauce

$\frac{3}{4}$ lb medium shrimps
$1\frac{1}{4}$ lb sole or flounder fillets
fat (for deep frying)

For fish croquettes
$\frac{1}{2}$ lb sole or flounder fillets, cooked and flaked
3 tablespoons butter
3 tablespoons flour
1 cup milk (infused with slice of onion, blade of mace, bay leaf and 6 peppercorns)
1 egg
salt and pepper

For coating
$\frac{1}{2}$ cup seasoned flour, made with $\frac{1}{2}$ teaspoon salt and pinch of pepper
1 egg, beaten to mix
$\frac{3}{4}$ cup dry white breadcrumbs

For fritter batter
$\frac{1}{2}$ package dry yeast or $\frac{1}{2}$ cake compressed yeast
$\frac{1}{2}$–$\frac{3}{4}$ cup warm water
$\frac{3}{4}$ cup flour
pinch of salt
1 tablespoon oil

For serving
fried parsley
lemon wedges
$1\frac{1}{2}$ cups Alabama sauce

Method

To make the fritter batter: soften the yeast in $\frac{1}{2}$ cup warm water. Sift flour into a bowl with the salt, make a well in the center and add the yeast mixture. Stir until smooth, adding more water if necessary to make a batter the consistency of thick cream. Add the oil and beat 2 minutes. Cover and stand in a warm place for 15 minutes or until well risen and foamy.

To make the fish croquettes: melt the butter in a saucepan, stir in the flour off the heat and strain on the infused milk. Blend until smooth, season and bring to a boil, stirring. Simmer 1–2 minutes and stir in the flaked fish, beating well. Take from the heat, beat in the egg and adjust seasoning. Turn the mixture onto a plate to cool.

Shape the mixture into small neat cylinders about $2\frac{1}{2}$ inches long, roll in seasoned flour, brush with beaten egg and coat with breadcrumbs.

Cut the uncooked fillets of sole or flounder in diagonal strips the size of a finger, roll in seasoned flour and coat with egg and crumbs. Toss the shrimps in seasoned flour and dip in the fritter batter.

Fry the croquettes and fish a few at a time in hot deep fat (350°F–375°F on a fat thermometer). Drain croquettes thoroughly on paper towels and keep fish hot while frying the remainder.

Mix all together on the same platter and garnish with fried parsley and lemon wedges. Serve Alabama sauce separately.

Alabama Sauce

Core, seed, chop and blanch 1 red or green bell pepper; drain and refresh. Stir into 1 cup boiled dressing (see Volume 4) with 1 clove of garlic, crushed, 2–3 stalks of celery, chopped, $\frac{1}{4}$ cup heavy cream, 2 teaspoons prepared horseradish and $\frac{1}{4}$ cup chili sauce or tomato ketchup. Season generously with salt, pepper, sugar and a dash of Tabasco.

Fritto misto includes deep-fried sole or flounder, shrimps and fish croquettes

Lobster Salad Valencia

2 live lobsters (1–1¼ lb each)
1 quart court bouillon (see box)
1 cucumber
salt
1 red bell pepper and 1 green bell pepper, cored, seeded and chopped
pinch of saffron, soaked in 2–3 tablespoons hot water for 30 minutes
1 cup rice
3 tomatoes, peeled, seeded and chopped

Method

In a kettle simmer lobsters in the court bouillon for 15 minutes and let cool in the liquid.

Peel and slice the cucumber, sprinkle with salt and cover; leave 30 minutes. Then rinse with cold water and drain. Blanch peppers in boiling water for 1 minute and drain.

Add the saffron liquid to 1 quart boiling water and cook the rice for 10–12 minutes or until just tender. Drain, rinse with hot water to remove the starch and spread out to dry in a warm place.

Cut the lobsters in half and discard the hard sac in the head. Remove the meat, including the green tomalley (in the body cavity) and any coral, and cut in neat pieces. Crack the claws and cut up this meat also. Mix the lobster meat with the cucumber, peppers, tomatoes and rice. Serve with Romesco sauce.

Court Bouillon

For 1 quart quantity: combine 1 quart water, 1 sliced carrot, 1 small onion (sliced and stuck with a clove), bouquet garni, 6 peppercorns, and 2 tablespoons vinegar or lemon juice in a pan with a little salt. Cover, bring to a boil and simmer 15–20 minutes. Strain and use.

Romesco Sauce

2 tomatoes
1 clove of garlic, peeled
1 large red bell pepper
4–5 whole blanched almonds, browned
salt and white pepper
½ cup olive oil
1 tablespoon wine vinegar (to taste) – optional

Method

Bake the tomatoes, garlic and pepper in an ovenproof dish in a moderately hot oven (375°F) for 20–25 minutes or until vegetables are soft. Discard the skin and seeds from the tomatoes and pepper and pound the flesh to a smooth paste in a mortar and pestle with the garlic and almonds. Alternatively, purée the mixture in a blender.

Add seasoning, then beat in the oil drop by drop with a whisk or in the blender. Add vinegar and adjust seasoning.

Leave the sauce ½–1 hour to mellow, then beat well before serving.

Poulet Olivade (Chicken Pie with Olives)

For pie pastry
1½ cups flour
pinch of salt
½ cup butter
1–2 tablespoons cold water

For filling
2 broiling chickens (2–2½ lb each), cut into 8 pieces each
¼ cup diced bacon
2 onions, sliced
1 tablespoon flour
3 large tomatoes, peeled, seeded and chopped
1 cup pitted green olives
1 tablespoon chopped parsley
salt and pepper

Deep 10 inch pie pan, or shallow baking dish

Method

Make the pastry dough and chill.

To make the filling: in a deep skillet heat the oil and fry the bacon until brown. Take it out, add onions and brown. Remove from pan, add the chicken pieces and brown on all sides. Stir in the flour, add tomatoes, olives, browned bacon, onions, and parsley and season to taste. Cover and cook over low heat for 30–40 minutes until chicken is tender. Remove it, turn up the heat and reduce the sauce, stirring, until very thick.

Arrange the chicken in the pie pan or baking dish and spoon the sauce over the top, leveling it as much as possible. Cool. Set oven at hot (425°F).

Roll out the pastry dough and lay it on top of the chicken. Trim the edges and flute them. Make a hole in the center of the pie for steam to escape. Shape leaves from the trimmings to decorate the center of the pie. Bake in heated oven for 10 minutes, lower the heat to moderate (350°F) and bake 20 minutes longer or until the pastry is brown.

Cheese-stuffed Peppers

6–8 small red or green bell peppers
2 cups creamed cottage cheese
1 tablespoon paprika
1 teaspoon thyme
1 teaspoon basil
½ teaspoon ground cumin
2 tomatoes, peeled, seeded and chopped
salt and pepper
1 cup sour cream (for serving)

Method

Core the peppers and trim the ribs and seeds, leaving the shells intact. Blanch them in boiling water for 3 minutes and drain.

Combine the remaining ingredients and season to taste. Fill the peppers with the mixture, arrange them in a buttered baking dish and bake in a moderate oven (350°F) for 25 minutes or until the peppers are tender. Serve with sour cream.

SCANDINAVIA

Iced Apple and Apricot Cream Soup

$\frac{1}{2}$ lb ($1\frac{1}{2}$ cups) dried apricots
5–6 tart apples, peeled, quartered and cored
$1\frac{1}{2}$ cups strong beef stock
1 bay leaf
few sprigs of parsley
2 stalks of celery, halved
2–3 cups water
salt and pepper
4 cups milk
$\frac{1}{2}$ cup heavy cream, stiffly whipped (for serving)

Method

Place apricots in a saucepan with the apples, stock, herbs, celery, seasoning and enough water to cover. Bring to a boil, cover pan and simmer gently for 20–30 minutes or until the fruit is soft. Remove the celery, parsley and bay leaf and work the soup through a fine sieve or purée in a blender.

Stir in the milk and season soup carefully. Thin it with more milk if necessary and chill. Spoon the soup into bowls, and top each with a spoonful of whipped cream.

Swedish Pickled Herring Salad

2 cups pickled herring pieces, drained
10–12 small new potatoes
$\frac{1}{2}$ cup vinaigrette dressing
1–2 dill pickles, thinly sliced
2 tablespoons chopped fresh dill

Method

Boil the potatoes in salted water with their skins on for 12–15 minutes or until just tender. Drain and peel them while still hot. Quarter or slice them according to size and moisten with the vinaigrette dressing. Cool.

Cut the herring into small pieces and mix into the potatoes with the pickles and more dressing if needed. Stir in the dill and pile the salad in a serving bowl.

Squabs in Cranberry Cream Sauce

4 squabs
2 tablespoons butter
1 shallot or scallion, finely chopped
1 tablespoon flour
$1\frac{1}{2}$ cups stock
salt and pepper
$\frac{1}{2}$ lb fresh cranberries and 2 tablespoons sugar, or 1 can (8 oz) cranberry sauce
$\frac{1}{4}$ cup heavy cream

Method

Set oven at moderate (350°F).

In a flameproof casserole melt the butter and brown the squabs slowly on all sides. Remove and split each bird in half; cut away the backbones.

Add shallot or scallion to the pot and cook slowly until golden. Stir in the flour, cook gently until brown and add the stock. Season and bring to a boil, stirring.

Replace the squabs in the pot and add the fresh cranberries and sugar or the cranberry sauce. Cover and cook in heated oven for 30–40 minutes or until squabs are very tender. Take out the squabs and keep warm. Work sauce through a strainer or purée it in a blender until smooth. Add the cream and taste for seasoning.

Replace the squabs in the casserole and pour over the sauce. Reheat in the oven for a few minutes before serving.

Peasant Girl in a Veil

2 lb Italian prune plums
$\frac{1}{2}$ cup sugar
$\frac{1}{4}$ cup butter
$\frac{1}{2}$ cup fresh white breadcrumbs
little sugar (for sprinkling)
$\frac{3}{4}$ cup heavy cream, whipped until it holds a soft shape
1 egg white

Method

Set oven at moderate (350°F).

Wash the plums and halve them, removing the pits. Lay them in a buttered baking dish, sprinkle with the $\frac{1}{2}$ cup sugar, cover with lid or foil and bake in heated oven for 25–30 minutes or until the plums are soft. Cool.

In a skillet heat the butter, add the crumbs and sprinkle with a little sugar. Fry until brown, stirring. Drain the plums and layer them in a glass serving bowl with the fried crumbs.

Whip the egg white until it holds a stiff peak and fold into the lightly whipped cream. Spread over the plums and chill thoroughly.

SOUTH AMERICA

Chilean Shrimp Chowder

1 dozen medium shrimps, shelled
2 tablespoons lard or oil
1 onion, chopped
1 clove of garlic, crushed
2 medium potatoes, peeled and diced
1 large tomato, peeled, seeded and chopped
1 tablespoon rice
¼ teaspoon crushed dried red pepper
½ teaspoon oregano
salt and pepper
1½ cups water
2½ cups milk
¼ cup crumbled Feta cheese

Method

In a saucepan heat the lard or oil and fry onion and garlic until brown. Add the potatoes, tomato, rice, dried red pepper, oregano, salt and pepper to taste and enough water to just cover the ingredients. Cover with a lid and simmer 15 minutes or until the rice and potatoes are almost cooked.

Halve the shrimps lengthwise and add to the chowder with the milk. Bring to a boil and simmer 2 minutes. Add the crumbled cheese, taste for seasoning and serve.

Escabeche de Gallina (Chilean Pickled Chicken)

3½–4 lb roasting chicken, cut in 8 pieces
¼ cup olive oil
1 cup dry white wine
1 cup cider vinegar or 1 cup more white wine
1 cup hot water
2 onions, cut in 8 wedges
3 carrots, cut in thick slices
2 medium turnips, cut in 8 wedges
2 stalks of celery, sliced
bouquet garni
6 peppercorns
salt and pepper
1 lemon, or 2 hard-cooked eggs, very thinly sliced

Method

In a flameproof casserole, heat the oil and brown the chicken pieces on all sides. Add wine, vinegar, water, onions, carrots, turnips, celery, bouquet garni and peppercorns. Bring to a boil, cover and simmer over low heat for 30 minutes or until the chicken is very tender. Cool slightly.

Arrange the chicken in a bowl, take out the bouquet garni and peppercorns and spoon over the vegetables. Taste the cooking liquid for seasoning, skim off any fat, and add to the bowl. Chill until set – the flavor will mellow if the dish is left for 24 hours.

Just before serving, decorate with very thin slices of lemon or hard-cooked eggs.

Salteñas

For pastry
2 cups flour
½ teaspoon salt
⅔ cup lard
4–5 tablespoons cold water
1 egg, beaten to mix with ½ teaspoon salt (for glaze)

For filling
½ lb ground beef
1 tablespoon oil
2 onions, chopped
1 fresh chili pepper, cored, seeded and chopped, or ½ teaspoon dried chili pepper
¼ cup tomato purée
1 cup cooked rice
¼ cup sliced, pitted green olives
2 hard-cooked eggs, peeled and diced
salt and pepper

Salteñas are the Bolivian version of a savory turnover, sold as snacks on street corners throughout the country.

Method

Make the pastry dough and chill. Set oven at hot (400°F).

To make the filling: heat the oil and sauté the onion with the fresh chili pepper until soft. Add beef and cook until brown. Add remaining ingredients, season highly and cook 5 minutes. Cool.

Roll out the pastry dough to ¼ inch thickness and cut four 7 inch rounds. Brush the edges with egg and pile the filling in the center. Lift the sides of the turnover so they meet in the middle and flute them firmly together. Make a small vent for the steam to escape, brush the turnovers with beaten egg and chill them at least 15 minutes.

Bake salteñas in heated oven for 10 minutes, turn down the heat to moderate (350°F), and bake 15 minutes longer or until the turnovers are brown and crisp. Serve hot or cold.

Pumpkin Fritters

1 cup cooked pumpkin purée
2 eggs, separated
2 tablespoons flour
¼ cup sugar
½ teaspoon ground cinnamon
pinch of salt
confectioners' sugar

For sauce
¾ cup honey
1 teaspoon lemon juice

Deep fat (for frying)

Method

Beat egg yolks into the pumpkin with flour, sugar, cinnamon and salt. Whip the egg whites until they hold a stiff peak and fold into the mixture. Drop the mixture a teaspoon at a time into hot deep fat (360°F on a fat thermometer) and fry a few fritters at a time until golden brown. Drain on paper towels, sprinkle with confectioners' sugar just before serving and serve with honey sauce.

To make the honey sauce: heat honey and add lemon juice; serve hot.

Papas con Aji (Potatoes in Hot Sauce)

4–5 medium potatoes
$\frac{1}{4}$ cup oil
2 cloves of garlic, crushed
1 medium onion, chopped
1 fresh green chili pepper, cored, seeded and chopped
1 cup milk
$\frac{1}{4}$ cup crumbled Feta cheese
1 tablespoon chopped parsley
salt and pepper
cayenne
1 hard-cooked egg, sliced

Serve these with hot or cold roast pork.

Method

Boil the potatoes in their skins in salted water for 15–20 minutes or until tender. Drain and peel them; cut in slices.

In a large skillet, heat the oil and fry garlic, onion and fresh chili pepper until brown. Add milk, then put in the potatoes and heat thoroughly.

Sprinkle the mixture with the cheese, parsley and salt, pepper and cayenne to taste and spoon into a serving dish. Decorate with slices of hard-cooked egg.

AUSTRALIA AND NEW ZEALAND

Avocado with Tomato Ice

3 avocados
1 medium can (1 lb) tomatoes
1 clove of garlic, crushed
1 onion, sliced
1 stalk of celery, sliced
$\frac{1}{2}$ teaspoon salt
2 tablespoons sugar
rind and juice of $\frac{1}{2}$ lemon
3 sprigs of mint
Tabasco and Worcestershire sauces (to taste)
1 egg white (if freezing in ice cube tray)

Serves 6 as an appetizer.

Method

In a saucepan heat the tomatoes, garlic, onion, celery, salt, sugar, lemon rind and juice, stirring until boiling. Press the tomatoes with the back of a spoon, then add the sprigs of mint. Cover pan and simmer 5–10 minutes. Remove the mint and work the tomato mixture through a nylon sieve. Cool it and add the Tabasco and Worcestershire sauces to taste – the mixture should be highly seasoned as freezing diminishes the flavor.

Chill the tomato mixture thoroughly and freeze it, covered, in an ice cube tray in the freezer. When almost firm, spoon the mixture into a bowl and beat 1 minute with a whisk to break up ice crystals. Whip the egg white until it holds a stiff peak, stir into the mixture and return it to the ice cube trays. Cover and freeze until very firm, whisking once more if the mixture has formed ice crystals. Mellow the ice by keeping at least 1 hour before serving to develop flavor.

To serve, lightly chill the avocados, cut them in half and remove the seed. Place a large scoop of tomato ice in the cavity and serve at once.

Avocado with tomato ice, an Australian dish, is a colorful appetizer

AUSTRALIA AND NEW ZEALAND
continued

Stuffed Fish

2 trout, sea bass or snapper (1½ lb each)
½ cup sherry
¾ cup milk

For stuffing
½ small onion, chopped
2 tablespoons butter
1 cup fresh white breadcrumbs
1 tablespoon chopped parsley
pinch of mixed herbs (thyme, dill, savory)
2 tablespoons hot water
salt
black pepper, freshly ground

In New Zealand, fresh water trout are the finest fish, caught in many of the lakes and rivers of both islands. This recipe is equally good for sea fish like bass.

Method
Wash the fish well, including the stomach cavity, dry, trim the fins and 'vandyke' the tail (cut in a 'v'). Place fish in a buttered casserole or baking dish, pour over the sherry, cover and refrigerate overnight.

Set the oven at moderate (350°F).

To make the stuffing: cook the onion in the butter until soft but not brown and add to the breadcrumbs with the parsley, herbs, hot water and salt and pepper to taste.

Drain the fish, reserving the marinade. Fill cavity of the fish with the stuffing, pour over the milk and reserved marinade, sprinkle with salt and pepper and bake in heated oven for 20–25 minutes or until the fish flakes easily when tested with a fork. Serve hot or cold.

Steak Diane

4 minute steaks
3 tablespoons butter
2 shallots or scallions, very finely chopped
2 tablespoons brandy or ¼ cup Marsala
1 tablespoon Worcestershire sauce
½ cup espagnole sauce (see Volume 2)
2–3 tablespoons tomato sauce
1 tablespoon chopped parsley

This famous dish was created in a well-known Australian restaurant. It is deceptively simple because although the cooking is done quickly at the table by the maître d', he uses a top quality espagnole sauce and fresh tomato sauce previously prepared behind the scenes in the kitchen.

Method
Heat half the butter in a large frying pan or chafing dish and when hot and foaming put in the steaks. Fry quickly on each side until brown. If the steaks have been cut thinly and beaten out with a mallet or rolling pin to three-eighths inch thickness, they should cook ½ minute on each side.

Add the shallots or scallions, pour brandy or Marsala into the pan, set alight and let the flames burn out. Add Worcestershire sauce, then the espagnole and tomato sauces. Simmer 1–2 minutes until thoroughly blended, add remaining butter, in small pieces, and the parsley. Shake the pan to blend the butter into the sauce without boiling, take from heat and serve at once.

Baked squash and parsleyed new potatoes are typical Australian accompaniments.

Simple Tomato Sauce

Melt ¼ cup butter in a saucepan, stir in ¼ cup flour until smooth and cook until straw-colored. Blend in 1 tablespoon tomato purée and 4 cups stock and stir until mixture boils. Add 1 large can tomatoes, crushing well with the back of a spoon, and stir in salt and pepper, 1 bay leaf and 1 clove of garlic, crushed. Cover pan and simmer 20–30 minutes. Work mixture through a strainer into a bowl, then use as required.

Carpetbag Steak

1½ inch thick sirloin steak
½ pint shucked oysters
¼ cup melted butter
juice of 1 lemon
1 tablespoon chopped parsley
salt and pepper

Poultry pins or trussing needle and string

This recipe is a specialty of Sydney, Australia, where oysters are plentiful and of top quality.

Method
Cut as large a pocket as possible in the steak. Drain the oysters, fill the pocket with them and sew up the opening with a trussing needle and string, or secure with poultry pins.

Brush the steak with melted butter, sprinkle with pepper and a little lemon juice and broil 7–10 minutes on each side for rare steak; transfer to a platter.

Heat the remaining butter until it is nut-brown and at once add the remaining lemon juice and the parsley with seasoning. Pour the butter over the steak and serve.

For tournedos steak, allow one steak for each person, stuff it with 2–3 oysters and cook as above, allowing 3–4 minutes on each side.

Pavlova, made of meringue, is filled with whipped cream and fruit

Pavlova

4 egg whites
$\frac{1}{4}$ teaspoon salt
1 cup sugar
4 teaspoons cornstarch
2 teaspoons vinegar
1 teaspoon vanilla
3 cups diced fresh tropical fruit in season – bananas, peaches, papayas, mangoes, pineapple
1 cup heavy cream, whipped until it holds a soft shape

8 inch springform pan

Method
Set oven at very low (275°F) and grease and flour the cake pan.

Whip the egg whites with salt until they hold a stiff peak. Add the sugar, 1 teaspoon at a time, beating until the mixture is stiff and shiny, then beat in the cornstarch, vinegar and vanilla.

Note: $\frac{1}{4}$ teaspoon cream of tartar is sometimes added instead of vinegar; both give a soft, sticky consistency to the Pavlova.

Butter a shallow baking dish and fill with the meringue mixture, hollowing out the center slightly. Bake for $1\frac{1}{4}$–$1\frac{1}{2}$ hours in heated oven, or until the meringue is very lightly brown. Cool slightly, then unmold and cool completely.

Just before serving, add sugar to taste to the lightly-whipped cream and fill the center of the Pavlova. Pile the fruit on top.

Pavlova
Both Australia and New Zealand claim the honor of creating this dish named for the famous Russian ballerina, Anna Pavlova (1885–1931).

An electric waffle iron ensures that heat reaches the top and bottom of a waffle evenly

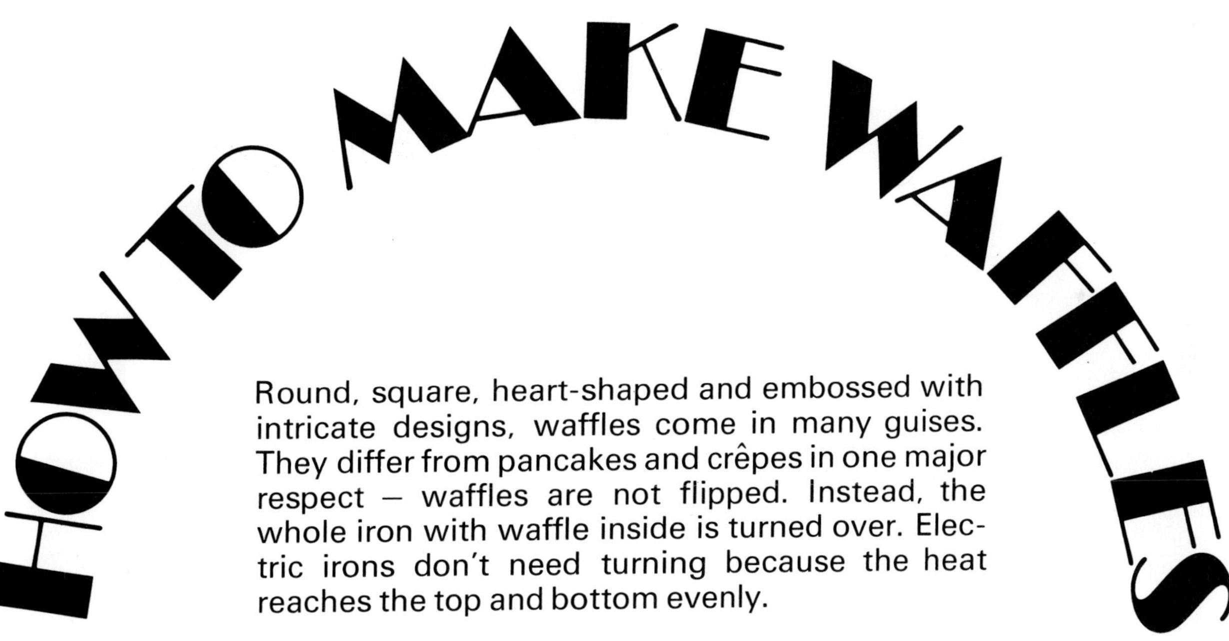

Round, square, heart-shaped and embossed with intricate designs, waffles come in many guises. They differ from pancakes and crêpes in one major respect – waffles are not flipped. Instead, the whole iron with waffle inside is turned over. Electric irons don't need turning because the heat reaches the top and bottom evenly.

Waffle Irons

Waffle irons were thought up by the French centuries before they became staples in American households. Such a splendid invention could not pass unnoticed and 'la gaufrette' soon spread north and south to Belgium and Italy. However, it was the Scandinavian countries that adopted waffles as a national dish and it is from Scandinavia that the finest non-electric waffle irons come today.

Heavy cast iron waffle irons are imported from Norway; these produce the classic heart-shaped waffle with deep impressions on both sides designed to catch a generous portion of sauces, maple syrup or melted butter. Generally, 4–5 hearts are arranged around the iron like the petals of a flower. The best of these irons come with a crown or ring to support them at the right height above the burner.

From Belgium comes another version of the classic iron – this time in a rectangle. It is made of **heavy cast aluminum** (that when dropped will not break like cast iron) but it does not distribute the heat as evenly as cast iron.

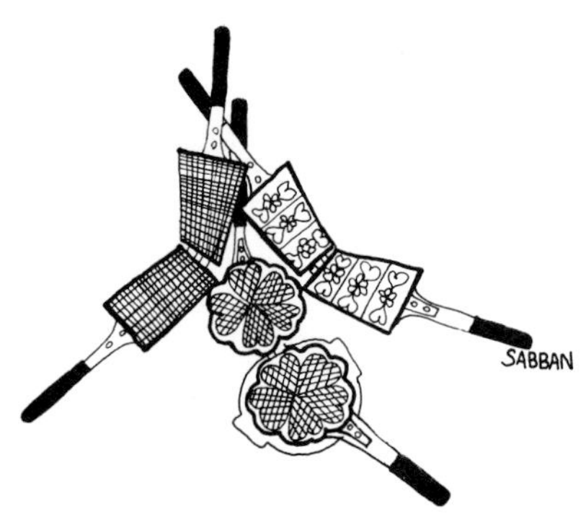

The Scandinavian **krumkake iron,** flat and circular, impresses its contents with a shallow, curlicued design on each side, sometimes with a religious or seasonal motif. The thin, crisp wafer it produces is quickly rolled while still hot to a cone-shape and can be served filled with whipped cream.

Goro irons, Norwegian in origin, produce three-part rectangular waffles or wafers; each section of the triptych is traced with a charming design. Goros are flavored with brandy, and they smell delicious while cooking. Serve as cookies.

Italians flavor their **brigidini** – crisp, wafer-thin waffles – with orange peel or aniseed and eat them as we do cookies.

The Swedish star-shaped **struvor iron** is dipped into deep fat, then into batter, and then into fat again, to make crisp brown rosettes that may be served with jam or cream or simply sprinkled with sugar.

Thick or thin, round or square, all waffles should be crisp and delicately browned and only a heavy iron that distributes the heat evenly will give you the right results. Follow the manufacturers' instructions when seasoning and using a new waffle iron; once seasoned, the iron should not be washed, but only brushed or wiped with a damp cloth to remove crumbs.

A new iron will tend to stick until it has been used several times, so grease it thoroughly and be prepared for a few failures before you achieve just the right balance of heat and consistency of batter. The perfectly crisp, delicately brown waffle is well worth waiting for.

Buttermilk Waffles

2 cups buttermilk
2 cups flour
1 teaspoon baking soda
2 teaspoons baking powder
large pinch of salt
2 eggs
6 tablespoons melted butter

Regular waffle iron

Makes 6 waffles.

Method
Sift the flour with the baking soda, baking powder and salt into a bowl. Make a well in the center and add the eggs and melted butter. Stir the buttermilk into the well with a whisk or wooden spoon and gradually draw in the flour. Stir until the batter is only just smooth.

Heat the waffle iron and pour the batter from a pitcher to cover about two-thirds of the iron. Close the iron, trim off excess batter and cook for about 4 minutes. The waffle is ready when the steaming stops. If the top does not lift easily, cook $\frac{1}{2}$–1 minute longer.

Serve with butter and honey or maple syrup, bacon, poached fruit or ice cream.

Cheese and Bacon Waffles

Fold $\frac{1}{2}$ cup grated sharp Cheddar cheese into the basic batter above. Pour into the hot iron and lay over 2–3 slices of bacon. Cook as for buttermilk waffles.

Nut Waffles

Sprinkle 1 tablespoon coarsely chopped walnuts or pecans over basic batter as soon as it is poured onto the iron. Serve hot with butter and honey.

Blueberry Waffles

Make as for buttermilk waffles. Serve with blueberry compote and sour cream or yogurt.

To make the blueberry compote: in a pan combine 1 quart fresh or frozen blueberries with 6 tablespoons sugar and $\frac{1}{4}$ cup water. Cover pan, cook over low heat for 8–10 minutes or until the fruit is soft. Mix 1–2 teaspoons arrowroot to a paste with the juice of 1 orange, stir into the blueberries and bring to a boil. As soon as the compote has thickened, take it from the heat and cool.

Chocolate Waffles

2 squares (2 oz) semisweet chocolate, grated
1$\frac{1}{2}$ cups cake flour
2 teaspoons baking powder
large pinch of salt
$\frac{1}{2}$ cup butter
1 cup sugar
2 eggs
1 teaspoon vanilla
$\frac{1}{2}$ cup milk

Regular waffle iron

Makes 6–7 waffles.

Method
Melt the chocolate on a heatproof plate over a pan of hot

water and leave to cool.

Sift the flour with the baking powder and salt. Cream the butter and beat in the sugar until light and soft. Beat in the eggs one at a time and add the vanilla. Stir in the chocolate. Fold in the sifted flour alternately with the milk until the batter is only just smooth.

Heat the waffle iron and cook as for buttermilk waffles.

Serve with ice cream, sweetened whipped cream or poached apples or pears.

Ginger Waffles

1 cup flour
1 teaspoon baking powder
$\frac{1}{2}$ teaspoon baking soda
1 teaspoon ground ginger
$\frac{1}{2}$ teaspoon ground cinnamon
$\frac{1}{4}$ teaspoon ground nutmeg
$\frac{1}{3}$ cup butter
$\frac{1}{2}$ cup water
$\frac{1}{2}$ cup molasses
$\frac{1}{2}$ cup dark brown sugar
1 egg, beaten to mix

Regular waffle iron

Method

Sift the flour, baking powder, baking soda and spices into a bowl.

Heat the butter with the water until melted, take from heat and stir in the molasses and sugar; let cool.

Make a well in the center of the flour mixture and add the sugar mixture with the beaten egg. Stir, gradually drawing in the flour, until the batter is only just smooth.

Heat the waffle iron and cook as for buttermilk waffles.

Serve with ice cream or lemon hard sauce.

Lemon Hard Sauce

grated rind of 1 lemon and juice of $\frac{1}{2}$ lemon
6 tablespoons butter
$\frac{1}{4}$ cup confectioners' sugar

Method

In a bowl cream the butter with the grated lemon rind. Add the confectioners' sugar alternately with the lemon juice, beating well after each addition. Pile in a small bowl and chill well before serving.

Gaufrettes

2 egg whites
$\frac{3}{4}$ cup confectioners' sugar
$\frac{1}{4}$ teaspoon vanilla
pinch of salt
$\frac{1}{2}$ cup flour
$\frac{1}{4}$ cup melted butter

Gaufrette iron; metal cone

Makes about 7 large wafers.

Method

Beat the egg whites until they hold a stiff peak and gradually fold in the sugar with the vanilla and salt.

Sift the flour over the mixture and fold in with the melted butter.

To cook gaufrettes, spoon the batter down the center of the iron, close it, trim off excess batter and cook until the wafer is golden on both sides, turning the iron during cooking.

If you like, shape the wafers into cones by rolling them around a metal cone while still hot. Spoon in the gaufrette filling, or serve plain or sandwiched with filling.

Gaufrette Filling

$\frac{1}{2}$ cup sugar
$\frac{1}{2}$ cup water
2 egg yolks
$\frac{1}{4}$ cup unsalted butter
1 tablespoon confectioners' sugar
2 tablespoons kirsch or rum, or 1 teaspoon vanilla

Sugar thermometer (optional)

Method

In a pan heat the sugar with the water until dissolved, then boil until the syrup spins a thread when a little is lifted on a spoon (230°F – 234°F on a sugar thermometer).

Beat the egg yolks until mixed, pour in the hot sugar, syrup, beating constantly, and continue beating until the mixture is cool – it should be light and very thick.

Cream the butter; beat in the confectioners' sugar and flavoring. Beat the butter into the egg mixture and continue beating until the filling is very light and fluffy.

Lemon Krumkakes

grated rind of $\frac{1}{2}$ lemon
3 eggs
$\frac{1}{2}$ cup sugar
$\frac{1}{2}$ cup melted butter
$\frac{1}{2}$ cup flour
Chantilly cream (for serving, see page 107) – optional

Krumkake iron; metal cone; pastry bag and a medium star tube (optional)

Makes about 25 krumkakes.

Method

Beat the eggs, add the sugar and beat until light and thick. Add the melted butter, mix well and stir in the flour and lemon rind.

Spoon or pour the batter onto the krumkake iron and press down the top; trim off excess batter. Cook about 30 seconds on each side or until golden, turning the iron during cooking.

Roll the hot krumkake around a metal cone and, if you like, pinch one end and fill with Chantilly cream, preferably using a pastry bag fitted with a star tube.

Above: spoon or pour krumkake batter onto the hot iron

Below: quickly roll hot krumkake around the metal cone

Italian Brigidini

2 cups flour
1 teaspoon baking powder
7 tablespoons butter
3 tablespoons sugar
1 teaspoon aniseed, or grated rind of 1 orange
2 eggs
5 tablespoons milk

Brigidini iron, or any round waffle iron such as krumkake

Makes 18–20 brigidini.

Method
Sift the flour and baking powder together into a bowl. Rub in the butter with the fingertips and add the sugar, aniseed, eggs and milk. Mix the batter until smooth.

Place 1 tablespoon batter on the iron, press down the top and trim off excess batter. Cook until golden on both sides, turning the iron during cooking. Serve as a cookie.

Sockerstruvor (Rosettes)

2 eggs
1 egg yolk
$\frac{2}{3}$ cup heavy cream
1 cup flour
$\frac{1}{3}$ cup sugar
deep fat (for frying)
confectioners' sugar (for sprinkling)

Sockerstruvor rosette iron

Makes about 20 rosettes.

Method
Thoroughly beat the eggs, egg yolk and cream. Sift the flour into a bowl, add the sugar and make a well in the center. Add the egg and cream mixture and stir in the flour to form a smooth batter. Cover and let stand 2 hours.

Put the head of the rosette iron in the cold fat, then heat fat to 370°F–375°F on a fat thermometer. Remove the iron and dip into the batter for a moment – do not let the batter run over the top of the iron; this makes it difficult to remove the rosette when cooked.

Dip the batter-coated iron into the hot fat and fry until golden – the rosette will slip off the iron when cooked. Lift out the rosette with a slotted spoon and drain on paper towels. Reheat the iron in fat and repeat. Serve rosettes sprinkled with confectioners' sugar.

Norwegian Goro

3 eggs
1 cup sugar
1 cup heavy cream
3 cups flour
$\frac{3}{4}$ cup melted butter
1 teaspoon ground cinnamon, or 1 teaspoon vanilla or brandy

Goro iron

Makes about 55 goro.

Method
Beat the eggs and the sugar together until light and thick. Add the cream, flour, butter and flavoring and beat until well mixed.

Spoon the batter down the center of the iron and press down the top, trimming off excess batter. Cook 1–2 minutes on each side or until golden, turning the iron during the cooking. When still warm, cut into thirds along the lines on the iron.

Dip the head of the sockerstruvor rosette iron into cold fat, then heat the fat and dip the hot iron head into the batter

Dip the batter-coated iron into the hot fat again to make a sockerstruvor rosette

Waffles

Crisp, golden waffles are (from left, goro, sockerstruvor rosettes and krumkake cones (recipe is on page 131)

MEASURING & MEASUREMENTS

The recipe quantities in the Course are measured in standard level teaspoons, tablespoons and cups and their equivalents are shown below. Any liquid pints and quarts also refer to U.S. standard measures.

When measuring dry ingredients, fill the cup or spoon to overflowing without packing down and level the top with a knife. All the dry ingredients, including flour, should be measured before sifting, although sifting may be called for later in the instructions.

Butter and margarine usually come in measured sticks (1 stick equals $\frac{1}{2}$ cup) and other bulk fats can be measured by displacement. For $\frac{1}{3}$ cup fat, fill the measuring cup $\frac{2}{3}$ full of water. Add fat until the water reaches the 1 cup mark. Drain the cup of water and the fat remaining equals $\frac{1}{3}$ cup.

For liquids, fill the measure to the brim, or to the calibration line.

Often quantities of seasonings cannot be stated exactly, for ingredients vary in the amount they require. The instructions 'add to taste' are literal, for it is impossible to achieve just the right balance of flavors in many dishes without tasting them.

Liquid measure	Volume equivalent
3 teaspoons	1 tablespoon
2 tablespoons	1 fluid oz
4 tablespoons	$\frac{1}{4}$ cup
16 tablespoons	1 cup or 8 fluid oz
2 cups	1 pint
2 pints	1 quart
4 quarts	1 gallon

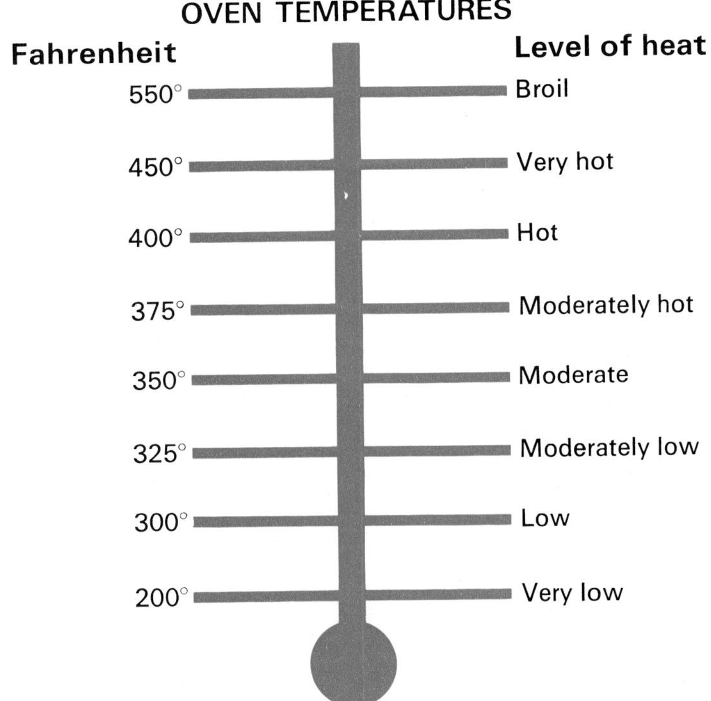

OVEN TEMPERATURES AND SHELF POSITIONS

Throughout the Cooking Course, oven temperatures are stated in degrees Fahrenheit and in generally agreed levels of heat such as 'high' and 'moderate'. The equivalents are shown on the table above.

However, exact temperature varies in different parts of an oven and the thermostat reading refers to the heat in the middle. As the oven temperature at top and bottom can vary as much as 25°F from this setting, the positioning of shelves is very important. In general, heat rises, so the hottest part of the oven is at the top, but consult the manufacturer's handbook about your individual model.

Pans and dishes of food should be placed parallel with burners or elements to avoid scorched edges.

When baking cakes, there must be room for the heat to circulate in the oven around baking sheets and cake pans; otherwise the underside of the cakes will burn. If baking more than one cake in an oven that has back burners or elements, arrange the cakes side by side. If the oven has side burners, arrange cakes back and front.

Oven thermostats are often inaccurate and are unreliable at extremely high or low temperatures. If you do a great deal of baking or question the accuracy of your oven, use a separate oven thermometer as a check on the thermostat.

A 14th-century scene showing a royal and diplomatic dinner – the King of Portugal (center) is entertaining John of Gaunt, who is on the King's right. Even at such royal occasions settings were simple – just knives and trenchers, forks not yet being in use. Bread played a main part in meals not only as a staple of the diet, but also to mop up food

Cooking Curiosities

The history of bread, originally a mealy substance, can be traced back to very early times. Flat cakes of flour and water dough baked unleavened (without any rising agent) were found in Early Hebrew, Egyptian and Chinese civilisations. From the *Book of Exodus* we know that after leaving Egypt the Jews had to live for a long time on unleavened bread because they had no yeast, and without it fermentation couldn't take place.

However, fermenting without yeast is possible and its discovery is attributed to the Egyptians. The mixture they used to leaven bread was made from sour flour left from the previous bread-making, and the must of grapes, that was kneaded with flour and then dried in the sun.

During the middle ages, bread trenchers preceded the advent of wooden plates for general use. The word trencher is derived from an old French word *trancher* meaning to cut, so a trencher is a cut slice of bread. The meat was carved on the trenchers and then at the end of the meal the bread was piled into baskets to be distributed to the poor. This gift of bread was not very enviable though, because stale bread some four days old was used for trenchers.

Even when wooden trenchers were used bread was still important to the meal as the diner would wipe his plate at the end of a course, then turn his plate over – a clean start for the rest of the meal.

The following verse is a modernised version of one that originally came from an early 15th-century manuscript, *The Book of Courtesy.* It describes the ceremony of laying the bread trenchers on the table:

Then comes the panter with loaves three,
That square are carven for trencher free,
Two set within and one without,
And salt-cellar covered and set en route;
With the overmost loaf it shall be set,
To make up the square, without let.
Two carving knives are placed soon,
The third to the lord, and also a spoon.

INDEX

(Volume 5)

B

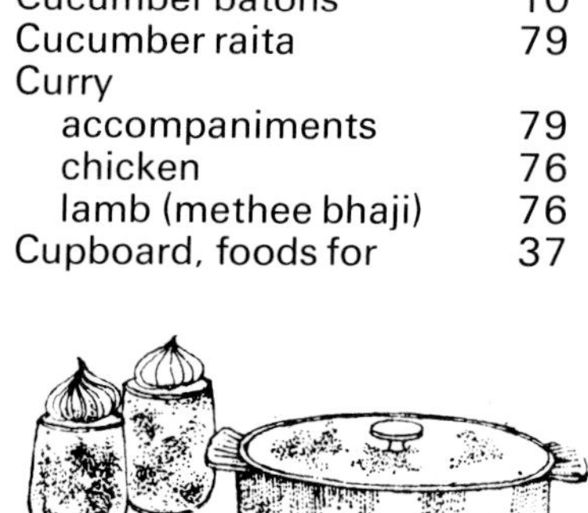

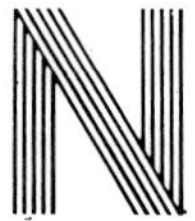

O

Index

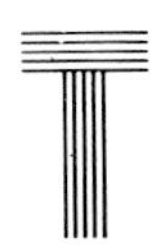

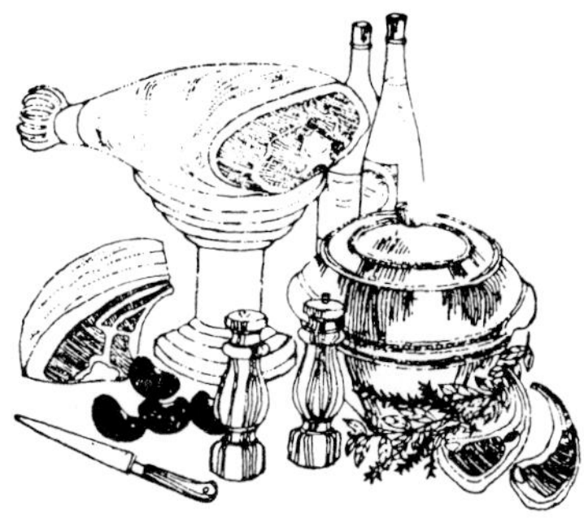

Acknowledgments
Photographs by Fred J. Maroon: pages, 8, 62, 66, 70, 89, 102, 131–133. Other photographs by Michael Leale, Roger Phillips, John Cowderoy and John Ledger. Photograph on page 16 by Pictor.